The
Vegetarian
Adventure
Cook Book

The Vegetarian Adventure Cook Book

By Rowan Bishop & Sue Carruthers

David Bateman

Publisher's note: The recipes on pages 120, 130, 131, 140 and 157 contain the ingredient gelatine. As this is an animal-based product, many vegetarians do not use it in cooking. Please substitute the same amount of agar-agar, a seaweed product, for gelatine if you wish to do so.

First published in 1988
Reprinted 1989, 1990, 1992, 1997, 1999, 2004

This edition published in 1996 by David Bateman Ltd,
30 Tarndale Grove, Albany, Auckland, New Zealand

ISBN 1 86953 261 9

Typeset by Typemakers International Ltd, Palmerston North
Cover design by Sue Reidy Design
Book design by Judith Kunzle
Printed in Hong Kong by Colorcraft Ltd

Preface

This book will allow you to sample dishes from cuisines around the world.

The recipes themselves are almost all original, using ingredients which are readily accessible to most people. Our aim was to create a useful book, as well as one to tempt and inspire those unfamiliar with meatless cooking. Thus the instructions are detailed and each recipe has been tested many times — they work!

In our experience, the biggest problem in planning a meal is finding what 'goes' with the main dish. This is why we have organised the recipes into menus, ranging from casual or family meals through to gourmet dishes. All the menus are nutritionally and aesthetically balanced, providing a harmony of nutrients and visual appeal.

This collection of recipes and menu suggestions demonstrates that a vegetarian diet is exciting, versatile and well within the reach of the average cook. We are convinced of the benefits of vegetarianism as a way of life, and our hope is that this book will inspire and encourage you to investigate the facts in detail for yourself.

We include the dessert section as an extra, because most people love desserts, and because in many cases the suggested dessert completes or complements the nutritional balance of the rest of the menu. They are not designed for the weight conscious, but, in moderation, a luscious dessert can provide a perfect conclusion to a memorable meal. All the menus can easily be complemented by a fresh fruit platter or salad, so we leave this to your discretion.

This book is for everyone, not just vegetarians. Above all, it's about enjoying food, on the way to a healthy and balanced life.

Note: All menus in this book cater for 4-6 people unless otherwise mentioned.

Acknowledgements

Firstly to Judith Kunzle, for illustrations, layout and cover design.
To our families, for their optimism and support over 10 months of researching, writing and testing.
Grateful thanks to the many friends in Rarotonga who helped and encouraged us.
Special thanks to those who tested recipes and contributed ideas.
This book was made possible only with support from those mentioned above; we hope that all those who use it gain as much pleasure as we did in compiling it.

Glossary of International Terms

Aubergines: Eggplant
Beetroot: Beets (the root).
Capsicum: Bell pepper, Sweet pepper.
Caster Sugar: Superfine sugar (Caster sugar can easily be made by putting Granulated sugar in the Food Processor with blade and blending until fine.)
Choko: Christophene
Cornflour: Cornstarch
Courgette: Zucchini
Icing Sugar: Confectioner's sugar, Powdered sugar
Kumara: Sweet Potato
Pavlova: A classic meringue dessert of New Zealand and Australia.
Silverbeet: A type of Spinach.
Tamarind: Pulp from seed of Tropical tree used to give curries, etc. a sweet/sour flavour.

Contents

MENUS
- Indicates preparation time (approximate)
  - • = 30 minutes or less
  - •• = 30 minutes to 1 hour
  - ••• = more than 1 hour

CONTENTS

CONTENTS

Kitchen Aids

Food Processor
We regard a food processor as an essential kitchen tool, and have geared our recipes accordingly. A blender, however, will suffice in many instances.

Microwave
Highly recommended, a microwave is a wonderful time saver for the busy cook. A basic model is fine, since you rarely need a very sophisticated one. We have not given specific instructions for microwaving, as the types and voltages differ so much. Get a good book, and learn how to use your own model; then you can adapt recipes to suit. Cooking times where given are approximate only, but based on a 600w model.
We tend to use a microwave for steps in the cooking process; this approach can be expanded according to individual preference. For example, we prefer not to microwave pastry or breads, but of course it is possible.

Wok
A wok is wonderful for stir fries, etc.

Pressure Cooker
This harmless but efficient aid is a marvellous help in the kitchen, especially if you don't have a microwave. (Cooking dried beans is simple with one of these.)

Steamer
You'll find a steamer very useful, mostly for vegetables.

Omelette/Crepe Pan
Keep this for one use only!

Measuring Spoons and Cups
These are essential. This book is geared to the use of level metric measures to ensure the most reliable results.

Knives
A range of sharp knives is necessary for any kitchen work, to facilitate and speed up preparation.

Wooden Spoons, Whisk, Set of Bowls and Saucepans
All these pieces of kitchen equipment are vital and make life much less complicated.

Electric Beater
This is necessary, although a small hand-held beater is quite adequate.

The Pantry Shelf

A well-stocked pantry can make meal preparation a real joy instead of a chore. There is nothing quite so frustrating as deciding on a recipe only to find that one or more of the essential ingredients is missing.

The following is a guide for stocking your shelves, especially for those who are new to vegetarian cooking. It's a good idea to collect glass jars with tight-fitting lids. Dried pasta, beans, dried fruit, grains and seeds make an attractive display stored in jars, and this storage method saves hunting around in the back of a dark cupboard.

Dried Beans

Aduki beans, black beans, broad beans, chickpeas, kidney beans, lentils, lima beans, mung beans, pinto and soya beans, split and whole peas.

Storage: Display in lidded glass jars. Store any excess in labelled clear bags in the freezer.
Cooked beans keep well in the freezer.

To cook beans: Beans should be washed well, then soaked overnight or for several hours. Use 3 times as much water as beans, and cook until tender, depending on the type of bean.
A pressure cooker is a great time-saver. Pre-soaking is not necessary. Wash and place in pressure cooker with 3-4 times as much water.

	Soak/Boil	Pressure Cook
Chickpeas	2½ hours	45-50 minutes
Pinto beans	1½ hours	30 minutes
Lima beans	1 hour	25 minutes
Kidney beans	1¼ hours	25 minutes
Split peas	30 minutes	10-12 minutes
Soya beans	3 hours	50-55 minutes

Refresh immediately under cold running water and drain. Beans can also be cooked, covered, in a microwave.

Seeds

Alfalfa seeds, pumpkin kernels, caraway seeds, poppy seeds, sunflower kernels, sesame seeds.

Storage: Store in glass jars for a limited time, as seeds do go rancid. It's best to store the bulk in the freezer in well-labelled bags.
Sprouted beans and seeds keep well in the refrigerator for up to a week.

Dried Fruit

Apples, apricots, currants, raisins, desiccated coconut, dates, figs, peaches, pears, sultanas.
Candied peel, crystallised ginger and cherries.

Storage: Display in a cool place in glass jars for up to 2 months. Store any excess in the freezer.

Grains and Flours

White flour
Self-raising flour

Storage: Keep in a container or jar for up to 6 months. Freeze any excess. Limited shelf life.

Wholemeal flour

Storage: Limited shelf life. Freeze excess in sealed containers or bags.

Arrowroot, cornmeal, cornflour, chickpea flour, soy flour

Storage: Good storage life if kept in well-sealed containers.

Wheatgerm, bran, rolled oats, bulghar or kibbled wheat, breakfast cereals, barley, etc. Storage as wholemeal flour.

Rice

White and brown.
Brown rice cooks very quickly in a pressure cooker. Place in the cooker with twice the volume of water and cook for 15 minutes.

Storage: White rice keeps well.
Keep a well-sealed jar of brown rice on display and freeze any excess to keep it from turning mildewed or rancid.

Nuts

Almonds, brazils, cashews, hazelnuts, macadamias, peanuts, pecans, pine nut kernels, walnuts.

Storage: Limited shelf life. Keep in well-sealed containers up to 1 month. Store excess in freezer. Check nuts carefully when purchasing, as they do tend to go rancid easily.

Dried Pasta

Cannelloni, lasagne, macaroni, noodles, spaghetti, rigatoni, tagliatelli, etc.

Storage: Excellent shelf life if kept well sealed.

Wholemeal pasta and buckwheat pasta

Storage: Limited shelf life. Store excess in freezer.

Tinned Foods

Artichokes, asparagus, bamboo shoots, beans and pulses such as soy beans, chickpeas, kidney beans, etc., beetroot, baby carrots, corn, green beans, mushrooms, tomatoes — whole peeled, puree and paste, savoury and tomato juice.
Vegetarian soups — handy for quick casserole and pasta dishes.
Vegetarian tinned nutmeats — good for rissoles and savoury bakes.
Vegetarian soya bean protein products — there are a variety on the market. We personally do not like the meat substitutes, such as burgers and sausages, so these products are not used in this book.

Fruit

Apples, apricots, blueberries, blackberries, blackcurrants, boysenberries, cherries, kiwifruit, gooseberries, guavas, lychees, mangoes, mandarins, passionfruit, pears, peaches, raspberries, strawberries.

Stored Goods

Although it's of course more desirable to use fresh vegetables, it's still convenient and practical to have a good range of tinned goods in the store cupboard, and frozen vegetables and fruits in the freezer.
Tinned vegetables have a shelf life of up to 2 years; tinned fruits have a shelf life of up to 1 year. Frozen fruit and vegetables may be kept for up to 1 year.

Herbs and Spices

It's a good idea to grow your own herbs, even if you only have a tiny balcony and no garden. Herbs will grow in a sunny, sheltered position in small pots, and young plants are available from most nurseries. Dried herbs, however, still have an essential place in the kitchen.

Herbs

Bay leaves, chives, dill, fennel, lemon grass, mint, marjoram, oregano, parsley, rosemary, sage, sweet basil, tarragon, thyme.

Storage: Keep in small jars away from heat and light. Shelf life is 2 months only, otherwise herbs can go musty. Keep any excess in the freezer.

Spices

Allspice, caraway, cardamom, anise, cayenne or chilli, celery seeds, cinnamon, cumin, fenugreek, five spice, ginger, mustard seeds, nutmeg, paprika, peppercorns, poppy seeds, saffron, tumeric.

Storage: Spices also go musty and lose their flavour after several months. Use up quickly and store any excess in the freezer.
Keep in the refrigerator in a sealed container after opening.

Tamarind is available in a dried, pressed form from oriental stores and some supermarkets. Soak in boiling water 15 minutes and then press liquid through a strainer. Good in curries.

Curry Powder

A recipe for making your own curry powder or garam masala can be found on p. 161. A good commercial curry powder is handy, though.

Condiments and Sauces

Salt, Mustard

There are now herb 'salts' available for those who wish to cut down on their salt intake.
A good variety of wholegrain mustards are now available.

Sauces

Apple, black bean, chilli or tabasco, soya, mint, horseradish, mayonnaise, tomato or ketchup, Worcester.

Peanut Butter

Peanut butter is of use in baking and also in oriental sauces and salad dressings. Buy a brand which has no added sugar.

Stock

It's a simple matter to make your own stock. Collect well-washed vegetable peelings except for onion skins and cabbage. Barely cover with water and simmer gently, covered, for 1 hour. Cool and strain. Freeze in covered containers.

Preserves

Jams and jellies, chutneys, capers, pickles and relishes, green peppercorns, green and black olives.
There are recipes in the miscellaneous section for making your own marmalade, chutneys, pickles and relishes.

Oils and Vinegars

Corn oil, soya bean oil, sunflower oil, nut oils and seed oils, olive oil.
There are a large variety of fruit, malt and herb vinegars available.
Buy the best quality oils. Nut and seed oils and olive are expensive, but well worth the investment. Make your own fruit and herb vinegars. Use plain wine vinegar and steep dried herbs or fruit in it for several weeks.

Other Flavouring Ingredients

Coconut cream (tinned), Marmite or yeast extract, instant soups and stocks, miso paste.

16

Baking and Desserts

Baking powder, baking soda, tartaric acid, dried yeast, dried milk powder, evaporated milk, condensed milk, honey, custard powder, vanilla and almond essence.

Cocoa and Coffee

As these are high in caffeine, you may prefer to use carob powder and bars available from health food stores.

Gelatine

As gelatine is an animal product, you may prefer to use agar-agar, a seaweed product with excellent setting properties.

White sugar, brown sugar, caster sugar, icing sugar.

Honey can be used instead of sugar if you wish.

Other Useful Items

There are now a number of 'long life' foods available which need no refrigeration until after opening. They include:

cream
milk
fruit juice
tofu (an excellent Japanese brand is now available)

These items have a shelf life of 6 months before opening. Note: Fresh tofu is readily available in most supermarkets and freezes very well.

Easy Measures for Common Ingredients

In compiling this book, we used level metric measures as our standard for all recipes.

Solids

	Cups	Imperial	Metric
Breadcrumbs (fresh)	1	2 oz	60 g
Butter or margarine	¼ cup	2 oz	60 g
Cheese (grated)	1½ cups	6 oz	180 g
Flour (sifted)	1 cup	4 oz	125 g
Lentils or beans (raw)	1 cup	8 oz	250 g
Nuts (chopped)	¼ cup	1 oz	30 g
Macaroni (uncooked)	1½ cups	6 oz	180 g
Rice (uncooked)	1 cup	6 oz	180 g
(cooked)	1 cup	6 oz	180 g
Sugar	¼ cup	2 oz	60 g
	1 cup	8 oz	250 g

Liquid Measure

The exact conversion is 1 pint = 568 ml. For easy reference it is recommended to convert as follows:
½ cup = 125 ml
1 cup = 250 ml
1½ cups = 375ml
2 cups = 500 ml
4 cups = 1 litre

The actual exact conversion is 1 oz = 28.35 g. For easy reference it is recommended to convert as follows:

1 oz = 30 g	2 oz = 60 g	4 oz = 125 g
6 oz = 180 g	8 oz = 250 g	10 oz = 300 g
12 oz = 360 g	14 oz = 425 g	16 oz = 480 g
1 kg = 2.2 lb.		

Fat Freddie's Pumpkin

**Florentine Pizzaz
(Entrée)**

**Celery, Apple and Nut
Salad**

Granny's Apple Pie

This most unusual centre dish really has to be tried to be appreciated. It's great to serve to guests, as it's quite a novelty; it also tastes wonderful and is so simple to prepare.

It can be served simply on its own, but the addition of a savoury flan entrée (with a salad for texture) and a dessert to finish makes a truly memorable meal.

We've given the recipes for 2 pumpkin weights here — one to feed 4-6 comfortably, and one to feed 6-8 with room to spare. The recipe can be adjusted for other weights in between.

Cheddar cheese is fine if gruyere is not available.

Any leftover pumpkin can be transformed into a soup the next day, made into pumpkin pie, etc.

This recipe is suitable for microwaving, but leftovers can be frozen for use as soup, etc.

Fat Freddie's Pumpkin

Thanks to Brigitte

1 whole pumpkin, 1-2 kg	**pumpkin, 4-5 kg**
1 tbsp oil	**4 tbsp oil**
2 tbsp margarine	**4 tbsp margarine**
3-4 thin slices of wholemeal bread	**7-8 slices**
1½-2 tsp yeast extract	**3-4 tsp**
1-1½ cups hot water	**1½ cups**
½-¾ cup sour cream	**1¼-1½ cups**
1 egg	**2 eggs**
1 tsp nutmeg, fresh grated or ground	**2 tsp, rounded**
salt and pepper to taste	**salt and pepper**
90-100 g grated cheese, ½ gruyere and ½ cheddar*	**200 g cheese**

Cut the top off the pumpkin to make a 'lid'. Scoop out the seeds with a spoon and discard.

Heat the oil and margarine together in a frypan. Dice the bread into crouton size and saute until golden brown. Drain, then pile into the pumpkin cavity.

Dissolve the Marmite in the hot water and pour into the pumpkin — this should fill the cavity about three-quarters full.

Beat the egg(s) with the sour cream, nutmeg and salt and pepper and add with the cheeses.

Stir gently to mix and adjust the seasoning if needed.

Replace the pumpkin 'lid' and place the filled pumpkin into a roasting pan.

Bake the smaller size pumpkin for 1-1½ hours, and the larger size for 2-2½ hours at 200°C. The flesh should easily admit a skewer when cooked.

Present the pumpkin whole at the table, scooping out the cheesy sauce with the flesh for each individual serving.

Florentine Pizzaz (Entrée)

Base

½ cup wholemeal flour
½ cup plain flour
½ tsp salt
50 g cold butter
⅓-½ cup milk

Topping

2 medium onions, skinned and
chopped
3 cloves garlic, crushed
2 tsp oil or butter
⅓ cup sour cream
300 g button mushrooms*
1 cup (approx.) grated
mozzarella or tasty cheddar
black or green olives for garnish

*Or use 200 g mushrooms,
thickened with 1 tsp cornflour
mixed with 1 tbsp water.*

Rub the butter into the flours and salt. Then mix the milk in lightly with a knife. (A processor may be used.)
Roll out onto a floured baking tray, thinly; it should cover most of an ordinary-sized tray.
Saute or microwave the onions and garlic, then the mushrooms, separately. Use 1 tsp butter or oil for each. Drain.
Spread the flan base with the sour cream, then spoon the cooked mushrooms over. Top with the cheese — and the olives if desired.
Bake at 200°C for approximately 25 minutes. Serve with the salad as an entrée to the pumpkin.

This recipe is unsuitable for microwaving. Freezes well, simply reheat in a hot oven.

Celery, Apple and Nut Salad

500 g celery, sliced thinly and on a diagonal
1½ apples, cored and quartered lengthwise, then sliced thinly
50 g walnuts, roughly chopped
¼ cup vinaigrette dressing (see p.165)

Sprinkle the apple with lemon juice after cutting to prevent browning. Mix the prepared celery and apple together in a serving bowl, pour over the vinaigrette and toss. Add the walnuts just before serving.

DESSERT

Granny's Double Crust Apple Pie
Page 128

Spicy Walnut and Rice Patties with Cheeky Plum Sauce

Kumara (or Potato) Salad

Crunchy Coleslaw

Mary's Chocolate and Orange Cream Pie

These quick and tasty patties can either be fried or barbecued. They're popular either way!

Try mozzarella for a different texture.

Not recommended for the microwave, these patties do, however, freeze well and can be reheated in an oven.

This sauce will be one of the quickest you've ever made, but it certainly doesn't suffer from this. It's so convenient to be able to produce such a smooth, rich, slightly oriental flavoured sauce with so little effort.

This recipe makes quite a big quantity, but any left over can be frozen. Alternatively, the quantities can readily be halved.

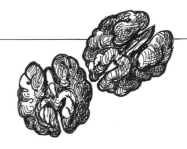

Spicy Walnut and Rice Patties

4 cups cooked rice, preferably brown
1 cup grated cheddar cheese, loosely packed*
1¼ cups toasted walnuts (or peanuts), chopped roughly
1 medium onion, skinned and grated
2 medium carrots, grated
¾ cup wholemeal flour
3 eggs, beaten
1 tsp tumeric
1½ tsp garam masala
2 tsp salt
1 tsp pepper
¼ cup cumin seeds mixed with ¼ cup wholemeal flour for coating.
If these are not available, use extra chopped nuts or sesame seeds.
4 tbsp oil for shallow frying

Mix the above ingredients, apart from the seeds and the oil, together in a large bowl.
Shape firmly into patties, using your hands.
Roll in the seed/flour coating mixture, then place in the refrigerator until needed.
Heat the oil in a heavy-based frypan, or lightly grease a barbecue plate. Cook the patties for several minutes on both sides.

Cheeky Plum Sauce

1 850 g tin Black Doris plums, with juice*
1 tbsp fresh ginger, skinned and chopped
1 tbsp soya sauce
½-1 tsp chilli sauce
1 tsp prepared mustard
4 tsp cornflour
2 tbsp cold water

Stone the plums. Then place the plum flesh and juice into a food processor or blender with the ginger, soya and chilli sauce and the mustard. Blend well.
Pour the mixture into a saucepan and bring to the boil, stirring occasionally (or microwave).
Mix the cornflour with the water. Remove the sauce from the heat while you pour the cornflour/water mixture into the sauce, stirring briskly.
Return to heat and bring back to boil.

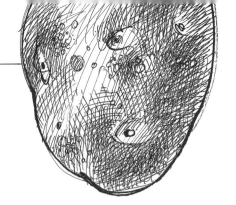

Kumara (or Potato) Salad

1 kg kumara (or potato)
1 tbsp vinaigrette dressing
¼ small onion, finely chopped
¾ cup sour cream
¾ cup cottage cheese
3 cloves garlic, crushed
2 tbsp lemon juice
1 tsp salt
pepper to taste
2 tbsp chopped spring onions
1 tbsp chopped parsley
Either: peeled, sliced orange if using kumara
or slices of fresh apple, sprinkled with lemon juice if using
potatoes
Grapes, diced celery, etc., are also a nice addition.

Dice the peeled kumara or potato into bite-sized chunks. Drop into boiling salted water and boil for approximately 4 minutes, so that they are very slightly undercooked (i.e. not mushy).

Drain and rinse thoroughly under cold running water, then drain again.

Place in a serving bowl and spoon the vinaigrette over, then carefully fork through the finely chopped onion. Take care not to break up the potato while doing this. Place in the refrigerator while you make the dressing.

Place the sour cream, cottage cheese, garlic, lemon juice and the salt and pepper in a food processor or blender. Blend until the mixture is smooth and creamy.

Pour the dressing over and through the salad, cover and refrigerate until needed. Just before serving, add the fruit if desired and garnish with the spring onions and parsley.

Kumara is a South Pacific name for a sweet potato.

Crunchy Coleslaw

Everyone has their favourite coleslaw recipe. For this particular menu, however, we suggest a very simple one consisting of finely shredded cabbage, diced celery and courgettes, grated carrot — and anything else you especially fancy.

Toss with the vinaigrette of your choice (see p. 165)

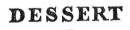

DESSERT

Mary's Chocolate and Orange Cream Pie
Page 130.

Carrot and Orange
Soup

Satay Rissoles

Ratatouille

Creole Salad

Old-Fashioned Bread
Pudding

Carrot and Orange Soup

2 tbsp oil
1 medium onion, chopped
1 kg carrots, scraped and chopped into small dice
1 tbsp finely grated orange rind
1½ cups fresh orange juice
1½ cups vegetable stock or 1½ cups water plus 1 tsp instant vegetable stock dissolved in it
½ tsp-1 tsp salt
¼ tsp freshly ground black pepper
⅛ tsp cinnamon
⅛ tsp nutmeg
natural yoghurt and finely chopped parsley for garnish

This soup is also very nice chilled, served with freshly made toast and butter.

This recipe freezes well.

In a large saucepan, heat the oil and gently saute the onion and carrots until the onion is clear.
Stir in the orange rind and juice, the vegetable stock, salt, pepper, cinnamon and nutmeg.
Bring to the boil, reduce heat and simmer until the carrots are very tender (or microwave).
Puree the soup in a food processor or blender until the mixture is very smooth.
Return to the saucepan and heat gently.
Serve in bowls with a swirl of natural yoghurt and a sprinkling of parsley.

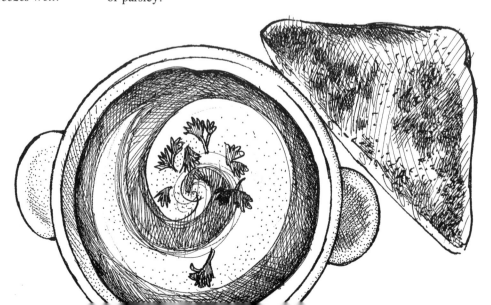

Satay Rissoles

1 medium onion, skinned and chopped
2 cloves garlic, crushed
1 tsp butter
2 eggs
2 tbsp lemon juice
2 tsp salt. pepper to taste
2 tbsp peanut butter
1 tsp chilli sauce
1 tbsp soya sauce
2 cups cooked soya beans (1 cup raw)*
¼ cup celery, diced very small
½ cup wholemeal flour**
2 cups cooked brown rice
1 cup grated cheddar cheese, loosely packed
¼ cup sesame seeds mixed with ¼ cup wholemeal flour for coating
4 tbsp oil for shallow frying

Saute or microwave the onion and garlic in the butter until the onion is soft. Drain and place in a food processor bowl with the next 7 ingredients. Mix well.
Now pour the mixture into an ordinary bowl and add the celery, the wholemeal flour, the rice and the cheese.
Shape into rissoles (using your floured hands) and coat with the sesame seed/wholemeal flour mixture. You should end up with 12 respectably sized rissoles. Refrigerate until needed.
Pour oil for shallow frying into an electric or ordinary frypan (or lightly grease a barbecue plate.) Cook the rissoles for several minutes on each side, until golden brown.

These rissoles are not only tasty but versatile, as they can either be cooked in a frypan indoors, or on a barbecue plate outside. Also, they can be made ahead of time and kept in the refrigerator until needed.

*Soya beans can either be soaked overnight, then cooked for approximately 3 hours or pressure cooked without pre-soaking for approximately 45 minutes. It's a good idea to cook up a reasonable amount of any bean you are working with, so that you can freeze any extra in appropriately sized batches.

** This is quite a soft mixture, but try not to add more flour, as this may detract from texture and flavour.

These rissoles are unsuitable for microwaving but freeze well.

23

Ratatouille

This is a version of the French vegetable casserole, variations of which now appear all over the world. It's a very popular dish and is almost impossible to get wrong, as the proportion of ingredients may be varied according to your taste and the availability of ingredients. It can be served hot, warm or cold, though not chilled. Ratatouille improves on standing and can be frozen for a later date.

If your aubergines are fresh, salting is not strictly necessary for this dish. You may, however, have to add a little water or stock to prevent sticking while your ratatouille is cooking.

2 medium-sized aubergines
salt
3 tbsp oil
3 medium onions, skinned and chopped
3-4 cloves garlic, crushed
6-8 chopped tomatoes
3-4 zucchini, sliced or cubed
2-3 red or green peppers, seeded and chopped
salt and pepper to taste
1½ tsp dried basil (1 tbsp fresh, chopped)
1 tsp dried or 1 tbsp fresh oregano
chopped parsley and olives for garnish

Slice and dice the unpeeled aubergines, sprinkle lightly with salt and leave to drain while you prepare the other vegetables.*
Heat the oil in a large heavy-based frypan. Saute the onion and garlic over a medium heat until soft.
Add the tomatoes, zucchini and peppers.
Next add the rinsed and drained aubergines, seasonings and herbs.
Cover the pan and turn the heat down. Cook slowly for approximately 30 minutes, or until the vegetables are the texture you prefer — they shouldn't be cooked to a pulp, though!
Sprinkle generously with chopped parsley and either black or green olives if liked.

Ratatouille may be cooked in a microwave if wished.

Serve Satay Rissoles and Ratatouille with natural yoghurt (a recipe for making your own can be found on p. 164).

Creole Salad

2 medium-sized, crisp apples
2 fresh pears
1 cup fresh, chopped pineapple or
2 bananas, chopped
1 tbsp lemon juice
½ cup plain yoghurt
1 tsp honey (runny or warmed)
torn lettuce or other salad green
2 tbsp toasted coconut

Chop the fruit into cubes or bite-sized chunks and sprinkle with the lemon juice.
Whip the yoghurt and the honey together with a fork, then pour over the fruit and combine.
Arrange the fruit mixture on a bed of torn lettuce or other salad greens, then sprinkle the toasted coconut over the top to serve.

DESSERT

**Old-Fashioned
Bread Pudding**
Page 135.

**Chilled Watermelon
and Cucumber Soup**

**Savoury Cheese
Charlotte**

**Avocado and Citrus
Salad**

**Grilled Tomatoes with
Herbs**

Eileen's Colonial Tart

Chilled Watermelon and Cucumber Soup

**3¾ cups fresh watermelon, peeled, seeded and diced small (about
½ small melon)**
**3¾ cups cucumber, peeled, seeded and diced small (about 3
medium cucumbers)**
¼ cup fresh orange juice
1½ cups natural yoghurt
1 tbsp fresh chopped mint leaves or good quality mint sauce

Place all the above ingredients into a food processor or
blender and process until smooth.
Pour into a bowl and place in the refrigerator until well chilled.
Serve garnished with a sprig of mint or chopped fresh chopped
parsley.
This soup does not freeze well.

So quick and easy, but
delicious, this recipe is a
life-saver if you want
something tasty but have very
little time.

**Variation
1½ cups sliced, lightly
sauteed mushrooms (about
350 g) or 1 cup whole kernel
sweetcorn or creamed corn in
place of the asparagus.*

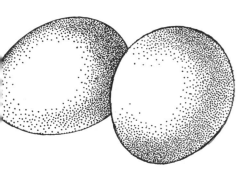

*This recipe is not
recommended for
microwaving or freezing.*

Savoury Cheese Charlotte

6 slices buttered wholemeal bread
1 350 g tin asparagus tips*
1½ cups grated cheddar cheese
4 eggs
1 tsp mild prepared mustard
2½ cups milk
1 small onion, peeled and grated
salt and pepper

Cut each slice of bread into 4 triangles and roughly line the
bottom and sides of a buttered 20 x 29 cm (8 x 12 inch) glass
baking dish, or a 20 cm (8 inches) souffle dish, buttered side
down. You should have 1½ slices of bread left.
Lay the drained asparagus tips over the bread triangles at the
bottom of the dish, then cover these with half of the cheese.
Top with the remaining bread and sprinkle over the remaining
cheese.
Beat together the eggs, mustard, milk and grated onion. Add
the salt and pepper to taste, then pour this over the prepared
dish.
Preheat your oven to 190°C.
Let the charlotte stand for 15 minutes.
Bake until it has puffed up and is nicely brown on top. This
should take approximately 45 minutes, by which time the
Charlotte should be firm to the touch.

Avocado and Citrus Salad

Any citrus seems to complement avocado perfectly, and this salad helps to stretch that precious avocado just a little bit further.

crisp green lettuce
2 medium grapefruit (or 2 large oranges)
1 large avocado
1 tbsp lemon juice
salt and pepper

Shred the lettuce and prepare as a 'bed' in a serving bowl, or platter.
Peel the grapefruit, including the white pith. Halve the avocado, remove the stone and skin, then slice.
Cut the grapefruit into segments and arrange the avocado and grapefruit on the lettuce bed.
Sprinkle with a little salt and lots of pepper, spoon over the lemon juice . . . and enjoy!

Grilled Tomatoes with Herbs

Allow 1 firm ripe tomato per person.
Cut in halves.
Sprinkle with a mixture of dried oregano, parmesan cheese, salt and pepper, allowing approximately ¼ tsp oregano and 2 tsp cheese per whole tomato.
Place under a hot grill until tops are browned or bake in a hot oven for 15 minutes.

DESSERT

Eileen's Colonial Tart
Page 133.

Hazelnut Loaf with
Mushroom and Cheese
Sauce

Potato and Onion
Souffle

Buttered Spinach or
Silverbeet

Swiss Plum Tart

This loaf is very easy to make, but tastes wonderful with a cheese and mushroom sauce.

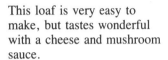

The easiest way to toast the nuts is to microwave them for 6 minutes with 1 tsp oil, stirring every 2 minutes, or pan fry with the oil until golden brown.

Hazelnut Loaf with Mushroom and Cheese Sauce

1 cup hazelnuts (or walnuts), toasted and roughly chopped*
1 cup fresh brown breadcrumbs
¼ cup wholemeal flour
½ cup rolled oats
4 tbsp milk powder
2 tbsp pumpkin kernels
¼ cup oil
2 medium onions, peeled and chopped finely
2 cloves garlic, crushed
1 small capsicum, seeded and finely chopped
1 medium carrot, grated
½ cup turnip, grated or cauliflower, finely chopped
2 cups zucchini, grated
1 tbsp fresh oregano, chopped or 1 tsp dried
2 tsp fresh thyme, chopped or ½ tsp dried
3 tomatoes, skinned and chopped, or the equivalent tinned
¾ cup boiling stock, preferably home-made
2 tsp yeast extract such as Marmite
freshly ground black pepper
½ tsp salt
½ tsp chilli sauce
1 tsp Worcester sauce
½ tsp nutmeg
½ tsp cinnamon
1 egg

Place the nuts, breadcrumbs, wholemeal flour, rolled oats, milk powder and pumpkin kernels into a large bowl and mix well.

Pre-heat the oven to 180°C.

Heat the oil in a pan.

Chop the onions, garlic and the capsicum in a food processor (don't mince), then saute gently until they soften.

Grate the carrot, turnip or cauliflower and zucchini (use the processor if you wish). Add these, with the chopped tomatoes and the herbs, to the other vegetables in the pan. Cook, stirring, for about 5 minutes over a medium heat. Add to the bowl of dry ingredients and combine.

Heat the stock plus all the stock ingredients together. Check the seasoning, then slowly pour the hot stock into the bowl with the dry ingredients and the sauteed vegetables.

Stir in the lightly beaten egg.

Line the bottom of a loaf tin with buttered greaseproof paper. Turn the well-mixed loaf ingredients into the tin, pressing down well.

Bake for 1¼ hours at 180°C, or until a knife inserted in the centre comes out clean.

Remove the loaf from the oven and let it sit for 5 minutes. Turn out onto a serving dish and top with the Mushroom and Cheese Sauce.

Garnish if desired with a little parsley.

This loaf may be microwaved and it freezes well.

Mushroom and Cheese Sauce

Make a bechamel sauce with 60 g (4 tbsp) butter, ⅓ cup flour, 1 tsp salt and pepper to taste and 2-2½ cups milk. Then:

1 cup sliced mushrooms
1 tbsp butter
2 tsp flour

Saute the mushrooms in the butter until tender. Stir in the flour, then gently add the bechamel sauce. Add:

½ cup tasty cheddar cheese, grated
¼ cup parmesan, grated

Adjust the seasonings and pour over the loaf.

29

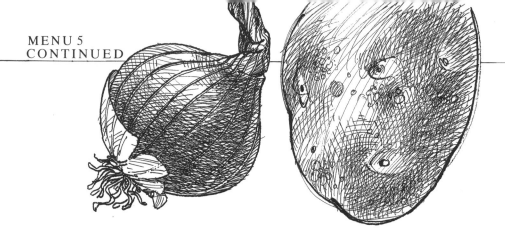

This souffle is easy and fail-safe.

Potato and Onion Souffle

500 g potatoes, peeled, cooked, mashed and kept warm
½ cup grated tasty cheddar cheese
1 tbsp chopped parsley
1 large onion, peeled and chopped finely
2 tbsp butter or margarine
½ tsp paprika
½ tsp nutmeg
2 tsp salt
1 tsp white pepper
½ cup sour cream or yoghurt
4 egg yolks
4 egg whites
pinch of cream of tartar

Pre-heat the oven to 200°C.
Combine the potatoes, cheese and parsley.
Saute the onion gently in the melted butter till soft, then add to the potato with the paprika, nutmeg, salt and pepper and the sour cream. (The souffle can be prepared to this point in advance. Warm through then proceed.)
Stir in the lightly beaten egg yolks.
Beat the egg whites until stiff but not dry and 'clumpy' adding a pinch of cream of tartar as they stiffen. Take care that the utensils are dry and that no egg yolk has slipped into the bowl.
Mix ¼ of the whites into the potato mixture to lighten, then carefully fold in the remaining whites.
Turn into a buttered 2 litre (3½ pint) souffle dish and bake for 30-35 minutes at 200°C, until risen and golden brown.
(This size dish will not need a "collar".)

Don't microwave or freeze this souffle.

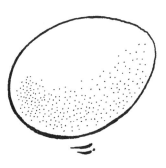

Buttered Spinach or Silverbeet

1 kg spinach or silverbeet, stalks removed
3 cups water
1½ tsp salt
1½ tsp grated nutmeg
3 tbsp butter
1 tbsp sour cream or yoghurt

Place the washed and chopped spinach in a large saucepan with the water and 1 tsp of the salt. Bring to the boil, then cook for 10 minutes or until tender.
Place in a colander and push out all excess liquid with the back of a spoon (save the liquid for making stock).
Stir in the remaining ½ tsp salt, pepper, nutmeg, butter and the sour cream.
Adjust the seasonings to taste.
Serve immediately in a heated serving dish.

This recipe is suitable for microwaving.

DESSERT

Swiss Plum Tart
Page 132.

Carrot and Walnut
Souffle

Quick Calabacitas

Eggplant Fritters

Pear and Raspberry
Upside Down Cake
with Chocolate Sauce

Carrot and Walnut Souffle

60 g butter
2 cloves garlic, crushed
5 tbsp plain flour
¾ cup milk
½ cup (125 g) sour cream
5 egg yolks
½ cup finely chopped walnuts
2 medium carrots, finely chopped
1 cup grated cheddar cheese, packed
1 tsp salt
freshly ground pepper
6 egg whites
pinch of salt
pinch of cream of tartar

Souffles are fun to make and a delight to eat. This one is an invention which worked first time and has, after many trials, never failed. Its flavour is guaranteed to win compliments. Add a crisp green salad for texture, dressed simply with a vinaigrette. You will need a 1 or 1½ litre (1¾ or 2½ pint) souffle or straight-sided dish. (The larger size will not rise much above the dish.) Most of the souffle can be prepared up to a day ahead if necessary, so there's no need for panic at the last moment.

This souffle is unsuitable for microwaving or freezing.

Melt the butter in a medium-sized heavy-bottomed saucepan. Saute the garlic over a gentle heat for 1 minute, then add the flour. Mix, then cook for 2-3 minutes before adding the milk slowly, stirring all the time. Add the sour cream and mix well, until the mixture is near the boil and thickened.
Remove from the heat and add the egg yolks, whisking well between each one.
Chop the walnuts in a processor, then do the same with the carrots (cut them into smaller pieces first). Add these to the sauce, along with the cheese, salt and pepper.
The sauce can be set aside at this stage, or refrigerated in a closed container if you're preparing a day ahead. Cover and refrigerate the egg whites also if you are pre-planning, but remember to allow them to return to room temperature before beating.
The sauce, too, should be reheated till warm (not hot) before it is needed.
Butter a 1 or 1½ litre (1¾ or 2½ pint) souffle or straight-sided dish, then take a piece of greaseproof paper long enough to fit around the outside of the dish, with a 5 cm (2 inch) overlap.
Fold the greaseproof in half, tie or pin it around the dish with the fold uppermost. Now turn up the folded edge 1 cm so that it acts as the rim of the dish.
Pre-heat the oven to 200°C.

The 'collar' of greaseproof paper should extend about 5 cm (2 inches) above the top of the dish.

Place the egg whites in a largish bowl, making sure that no water gets anywhere near them. If any yolk has slipped in, it must be removed.

A hand or electric beater can be used, but a wire whisk is our preference.

Beat the egg whites with a pinch of salt and a pinch of cream of tartar to stabilise (unless you have a copper souffle bowl) until the whites are stiff but not dry, i.e. you shouldn't be able to turn the bowl upside down, and the whites shouldn't 'clump'. Using a whisk gives more awareness of this crucial stage.

Mix about a cupful of the stiffly beaten whites into the warm sauce, then very carefully fold the rest of the whites in, until they are just mixed and no more — if you overmix, the souffle will not rise as much as you hope.

Pour into the prepared souffle dish, then transfer this to the pre-heated 200°C oven, which you should immediately turn down to 180°C.

Bake, without peeping, for 40-45 minutes.

Test with a skewer in the middle — it should be cooked but still a little moist (not wobbly).

Serve immediately.

33

This quick and popular dish originated in New Mexico.

Quick Calabacitas

1 tbsp oil
2 cloves garlic, crushed
3 small dried chillies, minced
1 medium onion, skinned and chopped
500 g zucchini, chopped into 1.5 cm (½ inch) chunks
1 medium tomato
450 g can of whole kernel corn, drained, plus half the liquid from it
1 tsp soya sauce
½ tsp salt
lots of freshly ground pepper
250 g grated cheddar cheese (2 very firmly packed cups)

This dish can happily be prepared ahead and reheated. Cooking times can be adjusted for microwave preparation.

Unsuitable for freezing.

   Heat the oil in a medium-sized saucepan, then saute the garlic, chillies and onion together over a gentle heat until soft. Add all the other ingredients except the reserved corn liquid and the cheese. Stir until all the vegetables are coated with oil. Add the corn liquid, bring just to the boil, then reduce the heat, cover and simmer for 15 minutes.
Add the cheese and simmer gently until the cheese melts. Place in a heated serving dish.

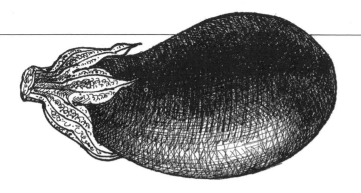

Eggplant Fritters

1 eggplant, 600-700 g
1 generous tsp salt
¼ cup plain flour
1 egg
¼ cup milk
1 cup dry breadcrumbs*
½ tsp salt
freshly ground pepper
⅓ cup oil, more if needed
sprig of parsley for garnish
lemon wedges if desired

Cut the unpeeled eggplant into 1.25 cm (½ inch) slices — these 'rounds' can be cut in half if you feel they are too big. Sprinkle them lightly with salt on both sides, using the first measure of salt. Leave to drain in a colander for about 30 minutes. (This step can be omitted, but salting removes any possible bitterness, and reduces oil absorption.)
Pat the eggplant dry with a kitchen towel or similar.
Lightly flour each slice, then dip into the egg beaten with the milk.
Now coat the slices with the dry, seasoned breadcrumbs.
Place the prepared fritters in a refrigerator for 30 minutes or more if time allows.
Heat the oil in a large, heavy-based frypan, then fry the slices for 3-4 minutes on each side, or until both sides are crisp and golden brown.
Drain on absorbent paper and keep hot until all the fritters are cooked.
Garnish with a sprig of parsley and lemon wedges if desired.

These fritters are suitable for freezing; simply reheat in a hot oven. Unsuitable for microwaving.

*Try adding some sesame seeds to the breadcrumbs.

DESSERT

Pear and Raspberry Upside Down Cake with Chocolate Sauce
Page 134.

Kumara and Zucchini Timbale with Green Peppercorn and Nut Sauce

Mediterranean Kebabs

Rainbow Salad

Fruit Compote

This attractively named dish provides an unusual and rather exotic focus for this meal, as its texture is reminiscent of the Middle Eastern couscous. Teamed with steamed rice, Mediterranean Kebabs and salads, it's a perfect choice for adventurous guests.
Note: Served alone, it would make a delightful entree for 6-8 people.

The tofu gives a more grainy, but very pleasant couscous-like texture to the timbale.

**The walnuts can be microwave/roasted in a bowl, without any oil or seasoning (about 6 minutes on high — stir every 2 minutes).*

This timbale may also be served at room temperature if you wish; it reheats very well, too, either in a microwave or in a conventional oven. May be frozen but reheat straight from the freezer.

Kumara and Zucchini Timbale with Green Peppercorn and Nut Sauce

600 g kumara (sweet potato), peeled
2 tbsp (30 g) margarine or butter
2 cloves garlic, crushed
½ tsp cumin
3½ tsp curry powder
¾ cup sour cream or cream
4 eggs
1 medium-sized zucchini, grated (unpeeled)
1 tsp salt
freshly ground black pepper
60 g tofu, mashed with a fork (optional)*

Sauce/Topping

45 g butter
1 tsp crushed green peppercorns (brine packed)
⅓ cup cream
50 g (½ cup) roasted walnut halves**

Halve or quarter the peeled kumara, then cook in boiling water until tender, about 20 minutes. Drain and allow to cool a little.
Melt the margarine or butter, then gently saute the garlic, curry powder and cumin in it for 2-3 minutes. Remove from the heat.
Pre-heat the oven to 180°C.
Place the kumara, the butter/garlic/curry mix and the eggs, cream, seasonings, zucchini and tofu (if used) in the bowl of a food processor. Process until smooth.
Pour the mixture into a ring tin which has been greased and the bottom lined with butter paper or buttered greaseproof.
Place the ring tin in a roasting pan with enough water in it to come halfway up the sides of the tin. Cover loosely with tin foil.
Bake at 180°C for about 40 minutes, or until the timbale is firm to the touch and has lifted away from the sides of the tin a little.
Leave to sit for a few minutes, then unmould onto a heated serving plate.
Serve with the sauce poured over and liberally garnished with the walnuts.

Sauce

Melt the butter, then add the crushed or mashed green peppercorns to it.
Reduce the heat, add the cream and stir until the mixture is well combined. Bring to the boil, then remove from heat.
Pour over the timbale and sprinkle the walnuts over the top.

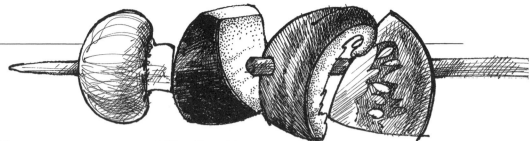

Mediterranean Kebabs

2 eggplants, 400-500 g each
salt
3 large green capsicums
3-4 medium-sized tomatoes
300 g mushrooms
salt and freshly ground pepper
⅓-½ cup oil

These colourful kebabs look and taste wonderful, and they're so simple and quick to prepare.
Cook them under a grill or on a barbecue.

Slice the unpeeled eggplants into 1.25 cm (½ inch) slices, sprinkle lightly with salt on both sides of each slice and leave to drain in a colander for at least 30 minutes. Pat dry, then cut each slice into quarters.
Remove the seeds from the capsicums, then cut the flesh into quite large chunks, about 4-5 cm (1½-2 inches) square.
Cut the tomatoes into quarters or eighths.
Leave smaller mushroom caps whole, or halve larger ones.
Pre-heat the grill to medium hot.
Thread the prepared vegetables onto skewers, sprinkle with salt and liberal grindings of freshly ground pepper.
Brush liberally with the oil, then place under the grill to cook. (Place about 8 cm (3 inches) beneath the grill.)
Grill, turning regularly and basting frequently with the oil, so that they don't burn or dry out. This should take about 15-20 minutes.

Rainbow Salad

400 g celery, sliced thinly
200 g (2 cups) mung bean sprouts
½ orange, peeled and sliced
1 cup sliced, fresh strawberries (or other fruit, such as grapes, apples, blueberries, etc., if strawberries not available)

Dressing
3 tbsp lemon juice
1 tbsp oil
1 tbsp honey
2 tsp whole seed mustard

You may also like to serve this menu with a plain lettuce salad.

Mix the celery, sprouts and orange slices together in a serving dish.
Shake the dressing ingredients together vigorously in a jar and pour over the celery/sprout mixture. Toss together.
Serve with the sliced strawberries sprinkled liberally on top.

DESSERT

Fruit Compote
Page 153.

Crepes can be an extremely useful and versatile basis for a meal, as they lend themselves to all sorts of variations depending on your particular whim — and what you happen to have in the cupboard. The essential ingredient, however, is a pinch of confidence; they're really a very simple and rewarding dish to make.

About 700 g silverbeet weighed with stalks.

Silverbeet and Mushroom Crepes

Wholemeal crepes
(makes approx. 10 crepes)

2 eggs
300 ml (½ pint) milk
¾ tsp salt
1 firmly packed cup wholemeal flour

Place all ingredients in a blender or processor, liquid ingredients first. Blend until smooth. This batter can be used immediately.

Place a heavy-based frypan, about 16 cm (7 inches) in diameter, over a moderate heat and grease it with a little oil or melted butter. When it is hot, pour in 2-3 tbsp batter and rotate the pan quickly so that the batter thinly coats the base of the pan. When bubbles have appeared and the batter has set, turn with a spatula or fish slice and cook on the other side. If the crepes have a solid, rubbery appearance, the mixture will need thinning with a little more milk.

Pile the cooked crepes on top of one another, ready for filling.

Topping

Make a thick white sauce using:

50 g butter
2 tbsp plain flour
1 cup milk
salt and pepper to taste
1½ cups mozzarella or cheddar cheese, grated

Melt the butter in a saucepan, add the flour, salt and pepper, then blend until smooth.

Gradually add the milk, stirring until the sauce thickens.
or
Using the same procedure, microwave in a deep-sided bowl or jug, stirring once after adding the milk, and cooking for 4 minutes.

Add ½ cup of the cheese, leaving the rest to sprinkle on top of the finished dish.

Filling

350 g fresh silverbeet, minus most of stalk*
150 g mushrooms, sliced
½ cup cottage cheese, mashed
2 cloves garlic, crushed
1 tbsp fresh chopped basil or 1 tsp dried
lots of freshly ground black pepper
salt to taste

The silverbeet, mushrooms, garlic and basil should be lightly cooked. With a microwave it's easy — simply wash the beet and chop roughly, discarding the thick rib of the leaves. Place in a bowl with the sliced mushrooms, garlic and basil. Add 1 tsp butter, then cover and cook 4 minutes.

Add a little more butter if cooking the vegetables in a pot. Drain the silverbeet/mushroom mixture then gently mix in the cottage cheese.

Check seasoning, then place about 2 tbsp of filling on one side of each crepe and roll up, folding in the ends. Place the rolled-up crepes seam side down in a single layer in a well-greased, ovenproof dish. (A dish measuring 29 x 20 x 4 cm (12 x 8 x 2 inches) is ideal.)

Pour over the sauce, then sprinkle with the rest of the grated cheese.

Bake in a pre-heated oven, 180°C for 30-40 minutes.

Variations

1. Use a 350 g tin of drained asparagus tips or chunks instead of the silverbeet, and 150 g of chopped peeled tomato instead of the mushrooms.
2. Saute 500 g diced aubergine (unsalted as long as it's fresh). Add 2 green peppers and 1 onion, sliced; 4 medium tomatoes, chopped; 1 tsp dried basil, salt and pepper. Simmer for 20 minutes, then thicken with 1-2 tbsp wholemeal flour mixed with a little water if necessary. Proceed as above.

This recipe is unsuitable for microwaving but it freezes well. Simply reheat in an oven.

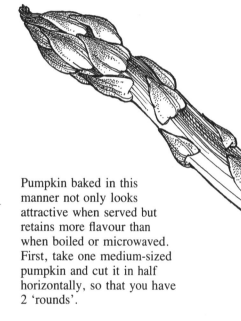

Baked Pumpkin

1 pumpkin round, approx. 1 kg
1 tsp butter
2 tbsp cream or top milk
pinch of nutmeg
1 dsp oil
1 tsp brown sugar

Scoop the seeds from the pumpkin half and place the butter, cream and nutmeg in the centre of it. Brush the rest of the pumpkin flesh, except the outside skin, with oil. Sprinkle the brown sugar over the flesh.

Now simply place in the oven at 180°C for ¾-1 hour, depending on the size of your pumpkin.

Slice at the table, garnished with a sprig of parsley.

Pumpkin baked in this manner not only looks attractive when served but retains more flavour than when boiled or microwaved. First, take one medium-sized pumpkin and cut it in half horizontally, so that you have 2 'rounds'.

Pumpkin can be cooked using this recipe in a microwave — this takes about 20 minutes — but our personal preference is for oven baked.

Green Salad

crisp lettuce, torn
fresh tomatoes, quartered
bean sprouts
slivers of gruyere cheese
toasted sunflower or pumpkin kernels

Toss the lettuce, tomato quarters and bean sprouts with a vinaigrette dressing (see p.165 if unsure) immediately before serving, then strew with the cheese and kernels.

DESSERT

Carrot Cake
Page 136.

**Mexican Corn Crepes
with Spiced Vegetables**

**Avocado, Tomato and
Onion Salsa**

Green Spinach Rice

Fresh Fruit salad

Serves 8-10.
This menu makes an inspiring
meal for a larger number of
guests. It combines unusual
textures, it's economical and it
tastes superb.
This menu and the Mexican
Frijoles (p. 44) combined
would make a wonderful
Mexican meal for a party of
about 20 people.

*The crepes, sauce, topping
and the filling can all be
prepared the day before; they
can then be assembled with
very little fuss on the day
they're needed.*

**The first crepe may stick —
if it does, wipe out the pan,
melt more butter and try
again.*

**The amount of chillies can
be reduced or increased
according to taste.*

Mexican Corn Crepes with Spiced Vegetables

Corn Crepes
(makes 20 crepes)
1 cup plain white flour
1 cup cornmeal
1 cup wholemeal flour
1 can cream style sweetcorn (310 g)
3 eggs
3 cups milk
1 tsp salt
1 tsp Worcester sauce
½ tsp freshly ground black pepper

Beat all ingredients except corn, preferably with an electric
beater, until smooth. The mixture is too large for a food
processor unless it is divided into 2 lots.
Stir in the cream style corn and let the mixture rest for 1 hour.
Using a small crepe or omelette pan with a 17.5-20 cm (7-8
inch) base, melt a little butter and heat until the butter sizzles.
Pour in approximately 4-5 tbsp of the batter and let it cook until
the crepes are bubbling on top and firm underneath. Turn with a
fish slice or spatula and cook until the other side is golden
brown.*
Cook up all the batter; grease the pan between cooking each
crepe by dropping about ½ tsp butter into the pan, then
removing from the heat to swirl the butter over the bottom. If
you are making the crepes in advance, pile them on top of each
other and cover them with plastic wrap. Refrigerate until
needed.

Filling

2 small onions, peeled and finely diced
2 small - medium potatoes, peeled and cut into small cubes
2 carrots, finely diced
2 capsicums, seeded and chopped very finely
2 tbsp butter
9 small fresh chillies, finely chopped (use gloves)*
or use canned jalapeno chillies or small dried chillies
2 tsp salt
freshly ground black pepper
2 tsp cumin powder
2 cups cottage cheese
1½ cups tasty grated cheddar

Saute all the vegetables in the butter until tender or
microwave on high for 3-4 minutes using only half the butter.
Stir in the seasoning and cumin.
Now combine the cottage cheese, cheddar cheese and the
vegetables in a bowl.

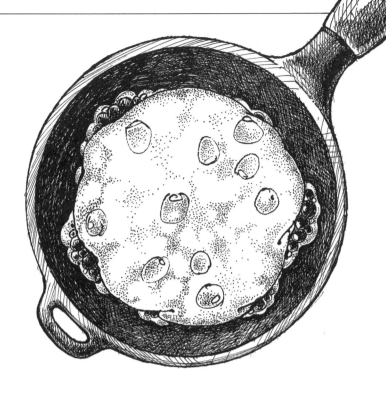

Topping

1 onion, finely chopped
4 cloves garlic, crushed
1 tbsp butter
2 425 g tins tomatoes (or savoury tomatoes)
2 tsp salt
freshly ground pepper
2 tsp brown sugar
2 tsp coriander
2 tsp tumeric
few drops tabasco sauce
olives, stuffed with pimentos
1½ cups sour cream
1½-2 cups tasty cheddar cheese, grated

Cook the onions and garlic in the butter until soft. Add the tomatoes with their liquid, then the salt, pepper, brown sugar and the spices.
Cook for 15 minutes, stirring occasionally or, using the same process, microwave, covered, for 7 minutes.
Heat the oven to 180°C.
To assemble the crepes place 2 tbsp or 1 very generously heaped tbsp of filling onto each crepe. Roll up and place in a greased baking dish, leaving a space between each one.
Cover the crepes with the tomato sauce topping, then place a spoonful of sour cream on top of each crepe and top with the cheddar cheese and a pimento-stuffed olive.
Bake at 180°C for 30-40 minutes or until the cheese is well melted and the crepes are hot and bubbly.

It's unlikely you'll have any, but leftover crepes freeze very well. Place the frozen crepes in a baking dish, then cook for 40 minutes in a pre-heated oven at 190°C.

41

Avocado, Tomato and Onion Salsa

*If there is no avocado available, a coleslaw would make a good accompaniment.

2 ripe avocados, peeled and cubed*
4 tomatoes, peeled and chopped
2 onions, finely chopped
juice of 2 lemons
salt and freshly ground black pepper

Combine all the above ingredients gently, seasoning to taste with the salt and pepper.
Chill and serve on a bed of crisp lettuce.

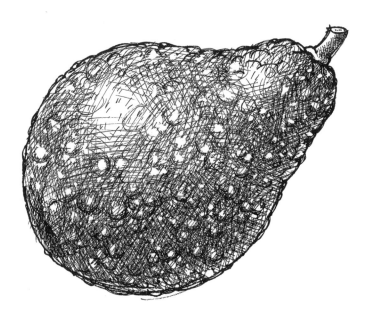

42

Green Spinach Rice

1 onion, chopped very fine
3 cloves garlic, crushed
⅓ cup oil
8 cups cooked brown rice, very well drained (4 cups uncooked)*
1½ cups cooked peas
1½ cups cooked spinach (300 g fresh leaves)
1½ cups of stock or 1½ cups water plus 1½ tsp instant green herb stock
¼ cup chopped parsley
freshly ground black pepper
3 tsp soya sauce
⅓ cup toasted sunflower kernels
green olives for garnish
2 lemon twists

The rice is actually better plain cooked the day before it's needed. The spinach and peas can also be cooked and set aside, ready for assembling.

Gently saute the onion and garlic in the oil. Stir in the rice till well coated with oil.

Now stir in the peas, spinach, stock, parsley, pepper and soy sauce. Let the mixture cook, stirring occasionally, for 5 minutes.

Serve heaped on a heated serving platter, sprinkled with toasted sunflower kernels and garnished with green olives and a twist of lemon.

DESSERT

Fresh Fruit Salad
Over to you.

Mexican Frijoles

Tortillas

Tapas

Tutti Frutti Ice Cream

Serves 6-8
A great meal for informal eating — Mexican beans and tortillas, with tapas. The only problem is that you usually eat far more than you need! Place everything on the table, provide everyone with a plate and a serviette for catching drops and dribbles— delicious.

This recipe is suitable for microwaving and freezing.

You will have to add more oil as you cook.

Mexican Frijoles

2½ cups dried pinto beans or a mixture of pinto, kidney and haricot
2 tbsp oil
2 medium onions, peeled and finely chopped
6-8 cloves garlic, crushed
8 small dried chillies, more if you're sure (crushed)
1 tbsp coriander
2 tsp tumeric
1 medium-sized green capsicum, seeded and diced
500 g fresh tomatoes, chopped or 1 425 g tin tomatoes, chopped, with juice
1 tsp dried oregano or 1 tbsp fresh chopped
1 tsp dried basil or 1 tbsp fresh chopped
1 425 g tin tomato puree
1½ tsp salt
1 tsp ground pepper
2 tbsp chopped fresh coriander (optional) or 2 tbsp chopped fresh parsley

Cook the dried beans, either by soaking overnight then cooking for approximately 1½ hours or pressure cooking, unsoaked, for 20-25 minutes.
Heat the oil in a large saucepan.
Saute the onions, garlic, chillies, coriander, tumeric and capsicum over a gentle heat until the onions have softened.
Add the chopped tomatoes, oregano, basil, tomato puree and salt and pepper.
Mix the cooked beans with the chilli mixture, cover and simmer gently for 10-15 minutes or pour into a casserole dish with a lid and allow the flavours to blend until ready to cook.
Reheat in an oven at 180°C for 30-40 minutes or until piping hot.
Garnish the dish immediately before serving with the fresh coriander (not ground) or parsley. (Fresh coriander is very commonly used in Mexican dishes, so would be more appropriate if you have access to it.)

Tortillas

1½ cups fine cornmeal
1½ cups wholemeal flour
1 tsp salt
1 cup warm water (approx)
3 tbsp oil for frying — more as needed*

Place the cornmeal, flour and salt in a bowl and mix.
Pour in the warm water, mixing quickly as you do this; the result should be a firm, but not stiff, dough. Shape the dough into a ball, then turn out onto a (plain) floured board.
Knead the dough lightly for about 4 minutes, adding a little more plain flour if necessary to prevent sticking.

The dough can sit for 30 minutes or so at this stage, but this is not necessary. Divide the dough into 14 pieces, shape each into a 'ball', then roll each ball into a thin circle, approximately 17 cm (6 inches) in diameter.

Heat the oil to medium high in a heavy-based frypan. Fry each tortilla for a few minutes on both sides, turning with a fish slice or tongs.

Drain the crisp, golden tortillas on kitchen paper, then place on a serving plate ready for the table.

Tortillas can be frozen while still fresh. Reheat in an oven.

Tapas

Serve them all or choose from:

1. A bowl of grated cheddar cheese.
2. Finely cut coleslaw or lettuce — serve mayonnaise separately.
3. A bowl of grated carrot, sprinkled with lemon juice.
4. A serving dish of sour cream.
5. Freshly cut tomato slices — and cucumber, if desired.
6. Sliced avocado, sprinkled with lemon juice.
7. A selection of olives.
8. Guacamole (p. 124) and anything else you fancy.
9. Chilli Fondue (for serving over/with, or dipping)

Chilli Fondue

2 tbsp oil
1 medium onion, peeled
4 small dried chillies, crushed or minced
3 large capsicums, green or red, seeded
4 medium-sized red tomatoes, skinned and chopped or 4 canned tomatoes plus ¼ cup juice
1 tsp salt
½ tsp freshly ground black pepper
1 tsp prepared mustard, such as Dijon
½ cup beer or wine (optional)
1 cup grated cheddar cheese
3 tbsp sour cream

Heat the oil in a saucepan over a medium heat.

Chop the onion, chillies and capsicums roughly, then place in the bowl of a food processor.

Don't blend to mush, but chop them small — use the pulse button to do this.

Saute in the oil until soft.

Plunge the fresh tomatoes into boiling water for a few seconds, then remove and peel them. Chop into dice and add to the pan with the capsicum/chilli mixture.

Add the salt, pepper and mustard.

Bring to the boil then turn the heat down.

Mix in the grated cheddar and the beer or wine; then simmer, uncovered, for 20-25 minutes. Stir in the sour cream and serve. This fondue can be microwaved.

DESSERT

Tutti Frutti Ice Cream
Page 138.

Eggplant Parmigiana

Semolina Gnocchi

Florentine Salad

Vanilla Ice Cream

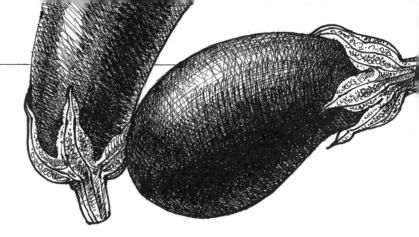

This famous Neapolitan dish is always a favourite, and served with Semolina Gnocchi and a Florentine Salad it makes a meal to remember.

Eggplant Parmigiana

2 largish eggplants (500-600 g each)
salt
½ cup flour
2 eggs, beaten
¼ cup milk
1½ cups fine dry breadcrumbs
1 425 g tin savoury tomatoes or whole tomatoes (plus juice) or
    500 g fresh tomatoes, skinned
1 425 g tin tomato puree
¼ cup oil, more as needed
2 cups fresh wholemeal breadcrumbs, seasoned (about 4 slices)
½ cup parsley, chopped finely
2 tbsp fresh basil or 2 tsp dried (or oregano)
250 g mixed mozzarella and cheddar cheese, grated
9 black or green olives for garnish
½ cup grated parmesan cheese

Slice the unpeeled eggplants into 1.25 cm (½ inch) slices. Sprinkle lightly with salt and leave to drain for 20-30 minutes. Dry with kitchen paper.

Dredge the eggplant slices in the seasoned flour, dip into the beaten egg/milk mixture, then coat with the dry breadcrumbs. Place in the refrigerator to firm the coating if time permits.

Mix the tomato puree and savoury together, and adjust the seasoning.

Heat the oil to medium high in a large frypan. Cook the eggplant on both sides until golden. Drain.

Place a layer of cooked eggplant slices on the bottom of a greased 30 x 20 cm (11 x 7 inch) baking dish or similar. You may have to cut some of the bigger slices in half or even into quarters to achieve an even layer.

Pre-heat the oven to 180°C.

Season the fresh breadcrumbs and mix these with the herbs.

Pour half of the tomato/savoury mix over the cooked eggplant. Sprinkle 1 cup of the breadcrumb mix over the sauce, then half of the grated cheese.

Repeat this process once more, then garnish with the olives, Sprinkle with the parmesan.

Bake for 40-45 minutes at 180°C (or microwave) or until the top is bubbling and golden.

This recipe will freeze very well.

Semolina Gnocchi

1 medium onion
1 bay leaf
4 cups milk
¾ cup semolina
1½ tsp salt
freshly ground pepper to taste
1 egg
1 cup parmesan cheese, grated or ½ parmesan ½ tasty cheddar
60 g butter
½ tsp dry mustard

Gnocchi are in fact Italian croquettes, and can be made from potatoes, semolina, cornmeal or spinach and ricotta cheese. These semolina gnocchi are simple to make and tend to enhance the flavour of the main dish rather than have a strongly distinctive flavour of their own.

   Peel the onion, cut in half and place in a saucepan with the bay leaf and milk. Bring to the boil, remove the onion and bay leaf, then slowly add the semolina, stirring all the time. Now add the salt and pepper.
Cook the semolina, stirring regularly, over a medium heat for 25-30 minutes until it is very thick — a spoon should stand up in it.
Remove from the heat, add the beaten egg and half the grated cheese, 15 g of the butter, and the mustard.
Spread the mixture into an oiled baking dish with sides so that it is about 1.25 cm (½ inch) thick. Leave to cool for an hour or more, until you are ready to shape into circles with a round cutter (or an upended glass).
Arrange the gnocchi in a single layer in a well-buttered baking dish and sprinkle with the remaining cheese. Melt the remaining butter and drizzle over.
Bake in a moderate oven, 180°C for 30-40 minutes, or microwave with time adjusted.

Florentine Salad

200 g spinach or silverbeet, stalks removed
1 small white or red onion, cut into fine rings
1 capsicum, seeds removed, cut into rings
10 black olives
½ cup toasted cashews or any other nut

   Shred or tear the spinach.
Place all the ingredients in a serving bowl and toss with sesame dressing (see p. 165).

DESSERT

Vanilla Ice Cream
Page 138.

47

Mediterranean Moussaka

Green Salad with Yoghurt Dressing

Tabouleh/Tomato Cups

Eastern Coffee and Spice Gateau

Mediterranean Moussaka

¾ cup brown lentils
1 cup water
2 medium eggplants, approx. 1 kg
salt
4 tbsp oil — more as needed
500 g potatoes (about 3 medium), peeled
3 tbsp tomato paste
1 425 g tin tomatoes plus juice
2 tsp chilli sauce (or to taste)
1 dsp Worcester sauce
½ tsp ground allspice
½ tsp ground nutmeg
1 tsp Marmite or similar yeast extract
½ cup stock (or water and ½ tsp instant stock)
1½-2 tsp salt (taste to be sure)
1 generous tsp freshly ground pepper (measured!)

This deliciously earthy dish combines well with tabouleh to create a distinctive Middle Eastern taste. Add lettuce salad with yoghurt dressing for texture and 'lift' and you have a most satisfying meal.

Simmer the lentils in the water for about 20 minutes (or microwave) until they are tender and the water has been absorbed. Set aside.

Cut the eggplant into 1.25 cm (½ inch) cubes, salt lightly and leave to drain for about 20 minutes. Dry on kitchen paper, then saute in the oil until lightly golden on both sides. Drain.

Cut the potatoes into 6 mm (¼ inch) slices. Saute or microwave in a little oil, covered, until just tender. Microwaving is ideal for this step, as the slices won't break up so easily.

Place the lentils in a food processor and blend with the tomato paste, tomatoes, Worcester sauce, spices, yeast extract, stock and seasoning.

Turn the oven to 180°C.

Place half the sauteed eggplant slices in the bottom of a greased dish, such as a lasagne dish or small roasting pan. One measuring 33 x 26 cm)13 x 10 inches) and 5 cm (2 inches) deep would be fine.

Pour half the lentil/tomato mix over the eggplant. Layer the potato slices in the middle, followed by the remaining eggplant and the last of the lentil mixture.

This recipe freezes well.

Top with the moussaka sauce and bake at 190°C for 40-45 minutes (or microwave).

Moussaka Sauce

4 tbsp butter or margarine
4 tbsp flour
2 cups milk
1 tsp salt
freshly ground pepper
2 eggs, separated
1 cup tasty grated cheese

Melt the butter in a saucepan. Add the flour and cook, stirring for a few seconds. Gradually stir in the milk, then remove from heat and beat in the egg yolks.
Beat the egg white until stiff, then fold it into the rest of the sauce with the grated cheese.
Pour over the rest of the moussaka and bake as directed above.

The recipe given above makes quite a thick layer of sauce, as it's delicious and a favourite part of the dish with everyone who's tried it. It can easily be halved, however, if you wish.

Green Salad with Yoghurt Dressing

fresh lettuce leaves, torn — enough for 4-6
1 cup plain yoghurt
2 garlic cloves, crushed
2½ tbsp cider vinegar
salt to taste
freshly ground black pepper
2 tsp honey

Place the prepared lettuce in a serving bowl.
Shake the remaining ingredients together in a jar with a lid and serve separately, so that guests can help themselves.

Tabouleh Tomato Cups

1 cup burghul (bulghur) or kibbled wheat
2 cups finely chopped parsley
¼ cup finely chopped mint
1 medium onion, finely chopped
¼ cup lemon juice (be generous)
4 tbsp oil (preferably olive)
1 tsp salt
freshly ground black pepper
tomatoes — 1 for each person*

Normally this recipe would contain 3 medium tomatoes, chopped, with juice and seeds discarded. These can be mixed into the salad before serving if the tabouleh is not to be served in tomato cups..

Place the burghul wheat in a bowl and cover with cold water. Leave to stand for 30 minutes. Drain well. Turn out on a kitchen towel and pat dry.
Place in a serving bowl, add the parsley, mint and onion.
Mix the lemon juice, oil and seasonings together, pour into the wheat and parsley mix and toss well. Place in a refrigerator to marinate for at least 1 hour.
Meanwhile prepare the tomato cups by cutting the stem end off the number of tomatoes required, then scooping out the flesh and seeds with a teaspoon.
Pile the tabouleh into each 'cup' for serving. Any extra tabouleh can be served on a bed of lettuce for selfserving.

DESSERT

Eastern Coffee and Spice Gateau
Page 137.

Turkish Pilaf

**Mediterranean
Casserole**

**Capsicum/Sesame
Strips
Pecan Pie**

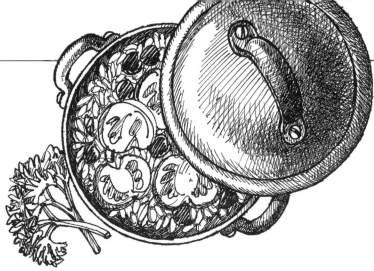

Turkish Pilaf is a quickly
prepared dish with a base of
eggplant and mushroom. It's
very like a tasty risotto, but
even simpler to cook.

*Brown rice may be used for
this recipe.*

Turkish Pilaf

1 large eggplant, 500-600 g
salt
2 cups white long grain rice*
⅓ cup oil, more if needed
1 large onion, peeled and chopped
150 g mushrooms, sliced — leave small ones whole
3 cups light vegetable stock or 3 cups water plus 2 tsp instant
mushroom or onion stock
2 tsp ground black pepper
1 tsp salt, optional — taste to be sure
4 medium-sized, ripe tomatoes, sliced
2 tbsp finely chopped parsley for garnish

   Cut the unpeeled eggplant into bite-sized pieces. Place in a
colander and sprinkle lightly with 1½ tsp salt then leave for 30
minutes to drain.
Pat dry on kitchen towels or similar.
Pre-heat the oven to 180°C.
Wash the rice until the water runs clear; this is important in this
particular recipe, as it plumps the rice out before cooking and
gives it a head start.
Leave the washed rice to drain while you saute the eggplant.
Heat oil in a large, heavy-based pan and saute the eggplant
pieces until they are lightly browned. Remove and keep aside.
Add a little more oil to the pan only if needed. Saute the onion
until it begins to soften, then add the mushrooms and saute
briefly.
Now pour in the stock, add the pepper and mix. Remove the
pan from the heat.
Pour the mixture into a large oval or round casserole dish with a
tight-fitting lid.
Add the cooked eggplant pieces and mix well, then check the
seasoning. Add the salt if required.
Sprinkle the uncooked rice evenly on top of the rest of the
ingredients.
Slice the tomatoes thinly and layer on top of the rice. Place on
the lid.
Place in the pre-heated oven and bake at 180°C for 40-45
minutes, without peeking.
Serve from the casserole dish, garnished with parsley.

*This dish is suitable for
microwaving if times are
adjusted.
Microwave approximately
35-40 minutes or pressure
cook 15 minutes.*

Mediterranean Casserole

Creamy, but piquant, with a light crunchy topping, this casserole combines perfectly with the pilaf.

250 g green beans, sliced lengthwise into strips and steamed or microwaved until almost tender
300 g chokos, peeled and halved around their equator, then sliced thinly and steamed or microwaved until almost tender. Cauliflower may be used instead*
3 tbsp butter or margarine
1 large clove garlic, crushed
1 medium onion, peeled and chopped
1 cup sour cream
1 cup grated tasty cheddar
1 tsp prepared mustard
1 tsp salt
1 tsp freshly ground pepper
1 tbsp extra butter or margarine
½ cup wholemeal breadcrumbs
1 tbsp parmesan cheese

*If using cauliflower, break or slice into small florets.

Turn the oven to 180°C. Heat the butter or margarine in a heavy-based frypan. Saute the garlic and onion until the onion is tender.
Stir in the green beans and choko slices and cook for 1-2 minutes.
Add the sour cream, cheddar cheese, mustard, salt and pepper. Mix well and cook for another minute.
Turn the mixture into a round casserole or souffle dish.
Melt the second measure of butter and toss with the wholemeal breadcrumbs and parmesan.
Sprinkle the breadcrumbs evenly over the top of the casserole and bake at 180°C for 20 minutes or until piping hot.

Capsicum/Sesame Strips

3 green capsicums
2 red capsicums
1 tbsp toasted sesame seeds
1 tbsp lemon juice
2 tbsp olive oil
½ tsp honey

Remove the seeds from the capsicums, then slice into slim strips, about 10 cm (4 inches) long.
Place in a serving bowl.
Mix the sesame seeds, lemon juice, oil and honey together, sprinkle over the capsicum strips and serve immediately.

This recipe is suitable for the microwave if it is finished off under a grill. It should not be frozen.

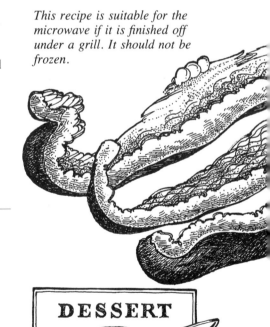

DESSERT

Pecan Pie
Page 140.

Chilled Apricot and Apple Soup

Egyptian Kusherie

Borani (Persian Salad)

Spicy Chickpea Salad

Dark Cherry and Almond Strudel

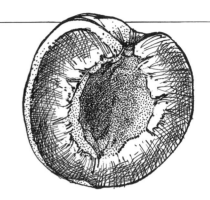

A quick and refreshing fruit soup.

Chilled Apricot and Apple Soup

1 820 g tin apricots with syrup or equivalent fresh stewed with liquid
3 medium-sized fresh tart apples, such as Granny Smith
2 stalks of celery, leaves removed
juice of 1 lemon
2 tsp grated orange rind (avoid the white pith)
juice of 1 orange
⅛ tsp ground ginger
⅛ tsp cinnamon
1 cup white wine or apple juice
1 cup natural yoghurt
chopped chives for garnish

Place the apricots, with their syrup, into a blender or food processor.
Peel and core the apples, chop roughly and add to the apricots.
Wash and roughly chop the celery and add to the processor.
Now add the lemon juice, the orange rind and juice, the ginger, cinnamon and wine or apple juice.
Process until completely smooth.
Put into a covered bowl in the refrigerator, and chill until it is very cold.
Serve the soup in chilled bowls with a good swirl of yoghurt in each and topped with a sprinkle of chives.

Egyptian Kusherie

Rice and Lentils

2½ tbsp margarine or oil
2 cups brown lentils
4 cups boiling water or stock (1)
2 tsp salt or to taste
½ tsp cinnamon
½ tsp nutmeg
2 cups uncooked rice
1½ cups boiling water (2)

Heat the margarine or oil in a large heavy-based frypan or saucepan, with a lid. Add the lentils and brown over a medium heat, for about 8-10 minutes, stirring often.
Add the boiling water or stock (1) and the salt, cinnamon and nutmeg. Cook uncovered for 10 minutes over a medium heat. Now stir in the uncooked rice and the boiling water (2), bring to the boil, then reduce heat, cover and simmer for 25 minutes without stirring (or microwave this step).

Sauce

1 365 g tin tomato paste
3 cups water
1 seeded, chopped capsicum
1 tbsp sugar
1½ tsp salt
1½ tsp cumin
1 tsp chilli sauce or ½ tsp cayenne
2 tsp Worcester sauce

Mix all the above ingredients together in a saucepan, bring the sauce to a boil then reduce the heat and simmer for 20 minutes (or microwave).

This is our version of an Egyptian rice and lentil dish given to us by an Australian friend. We recommend that this menu remain as such — the Borani and the Chickpea Salad perfectly complement the Kusherie, and a green salad adds colour and texture. This menu will serve 6-8.

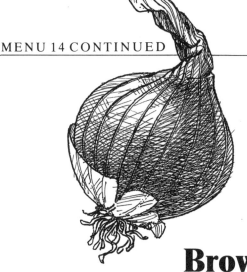

Browned Onions

3 tbsp oil
4 medium onions, skinned and sliced finely
5 cloves garlic, crushed
1 tsp sugar

Saute the onions and garlic in the oil until the onions soften.
Add the sugar and saute another few minutes until nicely
brown.
Remove with a slotted spoon to a serving dish.
To serve the kusherie, place the rice/lentil mixture onto a
warmed serving platter. Pour the tomato sauce over, then top
with the browned onions.
Garnish with parsley sprigs.

Borani (Persian Salad)

2 slim fresh cucumbers
2½ cups plain yoghurt
2-3 spring onions, finely chopped
¾ cup raisins or stoned, chopped prunes
½ cup walnuts
salt and white pepper to taste
1 generous tbsp finely chopped fresh mint or 1 tsp dried mint

Peel the cucumbers, halve lengthwise and, if very seedy,
scoop out. Slice thinly, sprinkle lightly with salt and leave to
drain for about 20 minutes or more.
Rinse cucumber, dry, then place in a serving bowl. Mix in the
yoghurt, then the rest of the ingredients.
Cover and chill for 1-2 hours.

Spicy Chickpea Salad

This salad is a favourite of ours.

1 small cauliflower or equivalent broccoli
2 cups cooked chickpeas
2 tsp tumeric
3 firm red tomatoes
1½ medium onions, peeled and finely chopped
½ tsp ground cumin
1 tsp salt, more to taste
1 tsp freshly ground pepper (measured)
¼ cup finely chopped parsley
3 tbsp oil, preferably olive
3-4 tbsp lemon juice

Break or slice the cauliflower into small sprigs.
Drop into boiling water and cook for 3 minutes.
Drain, refresh under cold running water, then drain again.
Toss the chickpeas and the tumeric together in a large bowl.
Add the cauliflower and toss again, taking care not to break up the cauliflower.
Cut each tomato into 8, then remove the seeds and discard. Add the tomatoes, onion, cumin, salt, pepper and parsley to the chickpeas and cauliflower.
Whisk the oil, lemon juice and extra seasoning to taste with a fork.
Pour the dressing over the salad ingredients and toss gently together before serving.

Try not to serve this salad too chilled, and if you are preparing ahead, add the tomatoes just before serving; refrigerated tomatoes tend to lose their freshness and become soggy.
If you are serving this salad without the borani, you may like to accompany it with natural yoghurt, served in a separate dish.

Green Salad

A green salad to accompany this menu needs to be perfectly plain, as the rest of the meal has lots of colour and texture. We suggest a simple spinach, or shredded lettuce/silverbeet salad, tossed with a plain vinaigrette.

DESSERT

Dark Cherry and Almond Strudel
Page 129.

**Silverbeet Soup
Supreme**

Mung Bean Muffins

**Cheese and Fruit
Platter/English Potted
Cheese**

Banana/Rum Crepes

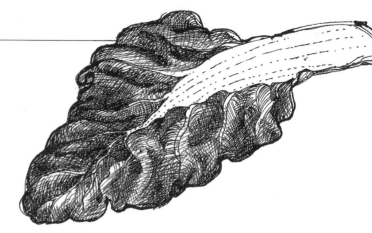

Soups are a rather sneaky but effective way of getting children to eat vegetables they normally won't touch. This soup's not just for kids, though.

Team this soup with mung bean muffins which, believe it or not, even children acknowledge to be 'scrumptious', and you have a quick but satisfying meal to appease and appeal to all appetites.

Present the soup and muffins with a Cheese and Fruit Platter, which can simply be a selection of cheeses and fresh fruits of the season. A potted cheese can be added to this, with chutneys and pickles if desired, and, of course, French bread.

Don't omit the yoghurt garnish, as this is the crowning touch for this lovely soup, providing a subtle tang.

We recommend that this soup is not microwaved or frozen.

Silverbeet Soup Supreme

**1 kg silverbeet, i.e. 450-500 g prepared leaves
6 tbsp margarine or butter
1 medium onion, skinned and finely chopped
6 tbsp plain flour
3 cups water with 3 tsp instant green herb stock added or 3 cups
vegetable stock
3 cups milk
½-1 tsp salt if needed (taste)
½-1 tsp freshly ground pepper
natural yoghurt as garnish***

Prepare the silverbeet leaves by removing most of the white stalks. Rinse, then shake dry and chop roughly. Place in a large saucepan, cover and cook for approximately 7 minutes, shaking or stirring occasionally. Don't add any extra water. Set aside.

Melt the butter in a saucepan, add the onion, and saute, stirring, over a gentle heat for about 3 minutes. Mix in the flour and cook for another 2 minutes.

Add the stock, cup by cup, stirring all the time, then 1 cup of the milk. Bring just to the boil, then remove. Add the other 2 cups of milk, mix, then allow to cool a little.

Add the cooked silverbeet to the soup, then puree in 3-4 lots in a food processor. Pour back into a large saucepan. The soup should now be a beautiful green, smooth and creamy. Taste and adjust the seasoning.

Reheat just before serving, but don't boil.

Present each bowl with a swirl of plain yoghurt (see page 164 for recipe).

Mung Bean Muffins

2 cups bran flakes
1 cup plain flour
1 tsp baking powder
¾ cup softened mung beans, i.e. soaked and sprouted for about 2 days.
¾ cup grated cheddar cheese
1 cup plain yoghurt*, generous
2 tbsp honey or golden syrup
1 tbsp brown sugar
1 tsp baking soda

The yoghurt may be replaced with milk, but your muffins won't be as light. We prefer these muffins oven baked rather than microwaved.

Pre-heat the oven to 200°C.
Mix the bran, flour, baking powder, mung beans and cheese together in a bowl.
Mix the yoghurt, honey, brown sugar and baking soda together and pour into the mung bean mixture (you may have to warm the honey slightly if it is creamed).
Fill well-greased muffin pans almost to the top.
Bake at 190-200°C for approximately 15 minutes.
Serve with butter and slices of cheese if wished, a sweet topping of your choice, chutney or whatever takes your fancy.

English Potted Cheese

This is a useful way to use up small quantities of leftover cheeses.
Sprinkle poppy seeds over the top of the cheese if you wish.

125 g butter
250 g assorted firm cheeses, grated, e.g. cheddar, gruyere, mozzarella, etc.
2 tsp prepared mustard
2½ tbsp port or sweet sherry
1-2 tbsp poppy seeds (optional)*

Beat the butter until soft, then mix in all the remaining ingredients until well combined.
Press into a pottery serving bowl (crockpot) if you have one — a ramekin dish will do — and refrigerate, covered, until needed.

DESSERT

Banana Rum Crepes
Page 141.

Minstrone Soup con Pesto

Yoghurt Bread

Neapolitan Salad

Peach and Blueberry Crumble

This deliciously nutritious soup can be quickly prepared, especially if you have some cooked brown rice on hand. In fact this whole menu is very quick to prepare. The bread contains no yeast, and so needs no rising — pop it in the oven and cook it at the same time as the crumble!

*If you are using tinned beans, a 300 g can is sufficient.

**Firm cooked noodles or macaroni may be used instead of rice.

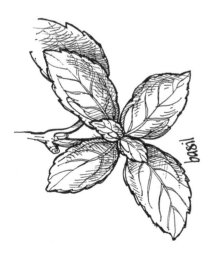

This soup may be cooked in a microwave, through all its stages. It freezes well.

Minestrone Soup con Pesto

2 tbsp oil
1 large onion, peeled and chopped
2 cloves garlic, crushed
1 large carrot, chopped into small dice
2 stalks celery, including leaves, chopped into small dice
1 420 g tin whole tomatoes, plus juice
1½ litres of vegetable stock or 1½ litres water plus 4 tsp instant green herb stock
1 bay leaf
1 tsp dried oregano or 1 tbsp fresh chopped
1 tsp dried basil or 1 tbsp fresh chopped
2 tbsp tomato paste
½ tsp yeast extract such as Marmite
2 tsp salt
1 tsp freshly ground black pepper
1 cup cooked kidney or haricot beans or chickpeas, (or tinned) plus ½ cup cooking liquid*
1½ cups firm, cooked brown rice**

Pesto

1 cup parsley sprigs, stalks removed or a mixture of fresh basil and parsley or silverbeet or spinach leaves
3 cloves garlic, crushed
½ cup parmesan cheese, grated
1 tbsp oil, preferably olive

Using an extra large saucepan (or bowl if microwaving), saute the onion, garlic, carrots and celery in the 2 tbsp oil until the onion is clear.
Add the tomatoes, stock, bayleaf, herbs, tomato paste, yeast extract and seasonings.
Cover and simmer for 30-40 minutes until the carrots are tender.
Add the beans with the ½ cup cooking (or tinned) liquid and simmer for 10 more minutes.
Stir in the rice, adjust the seasoning (be generous with the pepper) and cook for a further 2 minutes.
Place all the pesto ingredients into a food processor or blender, and process until pureed and very well combined.
Stir in the pesto and serve in bowls with extra parmesan if desired.

bay leaf

Yoghurt Bread

2 cups plain flour
2 cups wholemeal flour
¼ cup sunflower kernels or kibbled wheat
¼ cup wheatgerm or bran flakes
2 tsp salt
1 tsp baking soda
1 tsp baking powder
600 ml (1 pint) natural yoghurt
½ cup sprouted mung beans (optional)
1 tbsp sesame seeds for topping

Milk (500ml) may be used to mix this bread instead of yoghurt but it will not be quite as light.

Place all the dry ingredients into a large bowl.
Add the yoghurt and sprouted beans (if used) and mix well. The mixture should be neither too dry nor too sloppy.
Pour into a well-greased loaf tin and spread evenly. Sprinkle the top with the sesame seeds, then bake at 190°C for approximately 1 hour.
Turn out onto a cake rack, and allow 30 minutes, if possible, for it to cool.

Neapolitan Salad

50 g mozzarella cheese, chopped
3 hard-boiled eggs, quartered
1 small green capsicum, seeded and thinly sliced
3 medium tomatoes, quartered
1 small lettuce, shredded
6 black olives, stoned and sliced
1 medium onion, peeled and sliced into thin rings

Lay the shredded lettuce on an oval platter. Arrange remaining ingredients attractively on top.
Chill for 30 minutes before serving.

Dressing

½ cup vinaigrette
1 clove garlic, crushed
¼ tsp dried oregano or ½ tsp fresh chopped
1 tsp grated parmesan cheese
1 tsp finely chopped parsley

Shake all the ingredients together in a jar and pour over immediately before serving.

DESSERT

Peach and Blueberry Crumble
Page 142.

Spicy Pumpkin and Lentil Soup

Celery and Orange Salad

Corn Bread

Spinach Frittata

Lemon Meringue Pie

This soup is popular with both children and adults. It tastes delicious and is substantial enough to appease those traditionalists who believe that a soup's rightful place is as an entrée to a main meal.

Served with natural yoghurt, a crisp textured salad and corn bread, however, it makes a satisfying and balanced meal for a family dinner. If you want to make it more substantial, incorporate the frittata as well.

Don't omit the yoghurt; it's a perfect complement to this soup. A recipe for making your own yoghurt can be found on p. 164.

This soup may be microwaved and freezes well.

For a quick version, simply place all ingredients in a pressure cooker, except the first measure of water and the butter. Cook for 12-15 minutes. Blend if desired, or mash. Re-heat.

Spicy Pumpkin and Lentil Soup

¾ cup brown lentils
1 cup water
1 tsp cumin
1 tsp tumeric
2 tsp coriander
50 g butter
2 medium onions
1 kg pumpkin (about half a medium-sized pumpkin)
2½-3 cups water (some pumpkins are more 'solid' than others)
1 tsp salt
1 tsp onion, or green herb instant stock
2 tbsp tomato relish or chutney
freshly ground black pepper

Simmer the lentils, covered, in the water for 15-20 minutes (or microwave). At the end of this time, the water will have completely disappeared.

While the lentils are cooking saute (or microwave 1 minute) the cumin, turmeric and coriander in the butter until bubbling and aromatic.

Add the skinned and chopped onions, then saute (or microwave) until soft. Add the cooked lentils to this and mix well.

Skin the pumpkin and cut it into chunks.

Boil it with the 2½-3 cups water, salt and instant stock until tender. Add the tomato relish, then pour into a blender or food processor with the lentil/spice mixture. Blend thoroughly. You may have to do this in 2 or 3 lots.

Now pour the soup into a large saucepan, add freshly ground black pepper to your liking, and reheat. When the soup is piping hot, adjust the seasonings and pour it into generous serving bowls.

Garnish with natural yoghurt* and a sprinkle of parsley.

Celery and Orange Salad

3-4 cups celery, sliced in 1 cm widths on a diagonal
2 medium oranges, skinned and sliced into bite-sized chunks

Toss with a vinaigrette dressing, with added garlic and prepared mustard (see p. 165 if unsure).

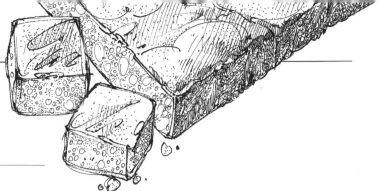

Corn Bread

1½ cups plain flour
2 slightly raised tbsp baking powder*
1½ tsp salt
½ cup wheatgerm
2 cups fine cornmeal
4 eggs, lightly beaten
2 cups milk
125 g softened butter or margarine

Sift the flour, baking powder and salt into a bowl. Stir in the wheatgerm and cornmeal.
Mix the beaten eggs, milk and softened butter together, then stir these into the dry ingredients, just until they are well mixed.**
Pour into a greased 33 x 23 cm (13 x 9 inch) swiss roll tin, and bake in a hot oven, 200°C, for approximately 40 minutes or until firm when tested with a skewer.
Cut into squares and serve warm, either plain or buttered.

The quantity given for baking powder is correct.

**The mixture is too much for most food processors to handle.*

This recipe makes quite a large quantity, but any leftovers can be split and toasted the next day for breakfast. Corn bread freezes well, too.

Spinach Frittata

350 g spinach or silverbeet, stalks removed
1 small onion, skinned and chopped finely
2 tbsp (30g) butter or margarine
½ tsp each of dried mint, basil and dill or 2 tsp each of fresh chopped
¼ tsp grated nutmeg
4 eggs
1 cup sour cream or yoghurt
½ cup milk
1 tsp salt
1 tsp ground black pepper
3-4 drops of chilli sauce
1 cup grated tasty cheddar cheese

Pre-heat the oven to 180°C.
Wash and chop the spinach, then steam for 5 minutes. Drain in a colander, pressing the leaves with a wooden spoon.
(Reserve the liquid for stock to use some other time.)
Saute the onion in the butter until tender, then stir in the spinach, the herbs and the nutmeg.
Grease a 30 x 20 cm (12 x 8 inch) or similar ovenproof dish, then pour the spinach mixture into this.
Beat the eggs with the sour cream, milk, salt and pepper, chilli sauce and half the cheese. Pour this on top of the spinach mixture in the dish.
Sprinkle the remaining cheese on top.
Bake at 180°C for 35-40 minutes, or until set.

You may like to add this very good but simple frittata to the menu for extra colour and balance.

This recipe unsuitable for microwaving or freezing.

DESSERT

Lemon Meringue Pie
Page 144.

Italian Pizza

Eggplant and Walnut Topping

Artichoke and Mushroom Topping

Cassata Ice Cream

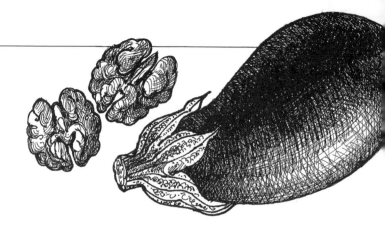

This recipe makes 2 pizzas 30 cm (12 inches) in diameter, or 1 45 cm (18 inches) in diameter.
We recommend using the 2 toppings for variety, one for each 30 cm pizza; or using both toppings for each half of the larger size pizza.

Pizzas are great for informal shared meals, and very easy too. Serve them on their own, or with a very simple green salad and French bread if you prefer.

Prepare the pizza dough, then, while it is rising, prepare the toppings.

Italian Pizza

Pizza Dough

1 cup warm water
3 tsp sugar
3 tsp dry granulated yeast
1 cup wholemeal flour
1 cup white flour
½ tsp salt
¾ cup white flour, extra

Dissolve the sugar in the water. Sprinkle in the yeast, then cover with a clean tea towel or cloth and keep in a warm place to allow the yeast to activate (about 10 minutes).
Place the flours and salt in a bowl. Mix. Add the yeast mixture, stir quickly, then place the dough into a mixer with a dough hook or knead by hand until the dough is smooth and elastic (not sticky).
Mix the extra ¾ cup flour into the dough while kneading.
Place the dough in an oiled bowl, covered with a clean cloth, then leave it to rise in a warm place for 1 hour.
When the dough has risen, punch it down, then turn it out onto a clean surface dusted with wholemeal flour and knead briefly.
Divide the dough in 2 if making 2 pizzas, shape into smooth balls and roll each out to about 1.25 cm (½ inch) thick to fit the pans or simply roll out and place on oven trays (greased).
Spread evenly with the sauce and one topping for each pizza, then bake at 200°C for 15-20 minutes.

Sauce

2 cups home-made Italian (Napoli — see p. 90) Sauce or 1 425 g tin of savoury tomatoes mixed with 2 tbsp chopped fresh basil (or 2 tsp dried) or fresh Tomato Sauce (p. 167)

Eggplant and Walnut Topping

1 eggplant, 500-600 g
6 tbsp oil
2 tbsp margarine or butter
4-5 cloves garlic, crushed
4 ripe tomatoes, chopped
1 capsicum, cut into chunks or strips (deseeded)
1 tsp salt
lots of freshly ground pepper
3 tbsp chopped walnuts (not too finely chopped)
¾ cup grated gruyere or cheddar cheese
¾ cup grated mozzarella

Slice the unpeeled eggplant into thin strips, about 5cm (2 inches) long.
Heat the oil in a large heavy-based frypan, then saute garlic for 2-3 minutes over a medium heat. Add the prepared eggplant, mix, then cover and cook for about 10 minutes, stirring regularly.
Add the tomatoes, the capsicum and the salt and pepper, then cook for another 5-10 minutes.
Spread on top of the sauce of one of the pizzas, or over half a large one. Sprinkle with the chopped walnuts, then the cheeses. Bake as directed above.

Pizza is unsuitable for microwaving but freezes well. Reheat from frozen in a pre-heated oven at 250°C for 10-15 minutes.

Artichoke and Mushroom Topping

2 tbsp oil
1 small onion, peeled and chopped finely
3 cloves garlic, crushed
1 small capsicum, seeded and chopped finely
1 tbsp fresh,chopped herbs such as basil or oregano or 1 tsp dried
½ tsp chilli sauce
salt and plenty of freshly ground pepper to taste
125 g sliced fresh mushrooms
2 tinned artichoke hearts, drained and quartered
¾ cup grated cheddar cheese
¾ cup grated mozzarella

Heat the oil in a heavy-based saucepan.
Saute the onion, garlic and capsicum until the onion is transparent.
Add the herbs, chilli sauce, seasoning and sliced mushrooms. Cook, stirring, for 2 minutes; the mushrooms should not cook down.
Sprinkle the topping on top of the pizza base, then place the quartered artichoke hearts on top of this.
Sprinkle over the cheese, then bake in a pre-heated oven at 200°C for 15-20 minutes.

DESSERT

Cassata Ice Cream
Page 138

This dish has wide appeal for all ages, so can confidently be served as a more casual or family meal.

1-2 tbsp pumpkin kernels may be pressed lightly into the surface of the prepared roll before cooking.

This recipe is not suitable for microwaving, but may be frozen.

Creamy Swedish Cabbage Roll

First Filling
2 tbsp margarine or butter
350 g finely shredded cabbage (prepared weight)
3 silverbeet leaves, destalked and finely chopped (optional)
½ cup sour cream
1 tbsp sugar
2 tsp white or wine vinegar
½ tsp salt
freshly ground pepper

Second Filling
½ cup grated cheddar
½ cup whole kernel corn
1 tsp prepared horseradish or chilli sauce

Scone Pastry
1 cup wholemeal flour
1 cup plain flour
½ tsp salt
3 tsp baking powder
4 tbsp (60 g) margarine or butter
¾ cup milk (approx.)

Melt the margarine measure of the first filling in a medium saucepan, then gently saute the cabbage, stirring regularly, for 5 minutes. Add the chopped silverbeet leaves and saute for 1 minute more. Remove from the heat.
Mix together the sour cream, sugar, vinegar, salt and pepper. Add to the cabbage mixture, mix well and set aside.
In a bowl, mix together the grated cheddar, the corn and the horseradish sauce. Set aside to cool. Drain off any clear liquid which appears.
To make the pastry, place the flours and salt and baking powder in another bowl.
Rub or cut the margarine or butter (or process) into the flour until it resembles breadcrumbs.
Add the milk and mix in — you should have a soft but not sticky dough.
Pre-heat the oven to 190°C.
Knead the dough 2-3 times on a floured board, then roll out onto an oven tray, so that a 30x 30 cm (12 x 12 inch) square is formed. Slide a long-bladed knife under the pastry, to ensure that it is not sticking.
Now spread the cabbage mixture evenly over the scone pastry, leaving about 3 cm (1 inch) around 3 of the edges. Brush these strips lightly with water, to seal.
Spread the corn/cheddar filling on top of the cabbage.
Starting from the end without a 3 cm strip, roll up as you would a swiss roll, pressing the side edges firmly together to prevent leakage, and ensuring that the roll lies seam edge down.
Bake at 190°C for 35-40 minutes.

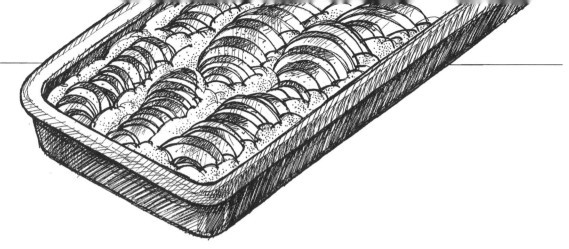

Potatoes Dauphinese

1 kg potatoes
1 tsp salt
freshly ground pepper
1 cup grated cheddar or gruyere cheese, or a mixture (generous measure)
1½ cups milk
2 tsp butter, chopped

Pre-heat the oven to 190°C.
Peel the potatoes, cutting the larger ones in half lengthwise.
Slice them thinly, into half rounds.
Butter a 20 x 30 cm (8 x 12 inch) or similar baking dish. Layer the potato slices into this, sprinkling in the salt, pepper and three-quarters of the cheese as you go.
Pour in the milk, then sprinkle the remaining cheese over the top of the potatoes.
Dot with the chopped butter.
Bake at 190°C for approximately 1 hour. The top should turn golden and crunchy, with creamy potato slices underneath.

This recipe is not recommended for microwaving or freezing.

Tomato Salad Provençal

500 g firm red tomatoes, sliced into rings just before serving
1 small onion, peeled and sliced into rings
8-10 black olives

Dressing

2 tbsp lemon juice
1 tbsp olive oil
1 tbsp finely chopped red capsicum (if available)
salt and freshly ground black pepper

Arrange the tomatoes, onion rings and olives in a serving dish, then pour the well-combined dressing over (don't toss).
Serve immediately.

DESSERT

Individual Meringues
Page 145.

65

Cream of Tomato Soup

Magical Courgette Bake

Jacket Potatoes

Sweet Baked Parsnips

Red Capsicum Salad with Snow Peas

American Fudge Brownies

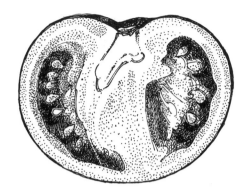

Cream of tomato soup is always popular, and this is a particularly quick and easy version.

This soup is very nice without the brandy, but its inclusion lifts this particular dish from the very nice to the superlative.

Cream of Tomato Soup

3 tbsp (45 g) butter or margarine
1 small onion, peeled and finely chopped
1 stalk celery, chopped
850 g red tomatoes, chopped or 1 820 g tin whole tomatoes
1 tsp brown sugar
1 tbsp chopped fresh parsley
¼ tsp dried sage or 1 tsp fresh chopped
¼ tsp dried basil or 1 tsp fresh chopped
⅓ tsp dried thyme or 1¼ tsp fresh chopped
1 bay leaf
1 tsp salt
1 tsp freshly ground black pepper
2½ cups vegetable stock, preferably home-made or 2½ cups water with 1 tsp yeast extract such as Marmite dissolved in it
2 tbsp flour
½ cup yoghurt
½ cup sour cream
⅛ cup brandy (optional)*

Melt 1 tbsp of the butter in a pan or saucepan and saute gently until clear.
Add the tomatoes, sugar, herbs, bay leaf and seasonings and cook for 3 minutes.
Add the vegetable stock, cover and simmer for 20 minutes. Recipe may be microwaved up to this stage.
Strain the mixture into a bowl, pressing down well with a wooden spoon to extract as much liquid as possible.
In a medium saucepan, melt the remaining 2 tbsp butter, then remove the pan from the heat and stir in the flour to make a smooth roux.
Add a little tomato mixture and stir well.
Return the pan to the heat and very slowly add the remaining tomato mixture, stirring constantly until just on the boil. (The mixture could be cooled and frozen at this stage. Reheat gently.)
Remove from the heat, then add a little of the tomato mixture to the mixed sour cream and yoghurt. Slowly mix this into the rest of the soup.
Add the brandy (if used) and reheat carefully to serve.

Magical Courgette Bake

450 g courgettes, grated (about 4 medium)*
5 eggs
2 cups milk
½ cup cottage cheese
¾ cup wholemeal flour
1 tsp baking powder
2 tsp salt
lots of freshly ground black pepper
1 cup grated tasty cheese
¼ cup pumpkin kernels

Grate the courgettes, then sprinkle with salt and leave to drain for 15-20 minutes if possible. Squeeze out excess moisture before using.

Pre-heat the oven to 190°C.

Place the eggs, milk, cottage cheese, flour, baking powder and salt into a food processor (metal blade). Process briefly.

Add three-quarters of the cheese, and the squeezed courgettes. Process just to mix through.

Pour into a greased 30 x 20 cm (12 x 8 inch) baking dish or similar.

Sprinkle with the remaining cheese and the pumpkin kernels. Bake at 190°C for 45 minutes.

We call this dish 'magical' because you just mix all the ingredients together, pour it into a baking dish and it forms its own 'crust' base. So easy!

The filling resembles a firm, textured souffle.

We recommend courgettes but give 2 alternatives which are just as good. This dish seems to be foolproof.

*Instead of courgettes, use 1¼ cups leftover baked pumpkin, mashed dry or 1¼ cups grated carrot.

This recipe is not suited to microwaving or freezing.

67

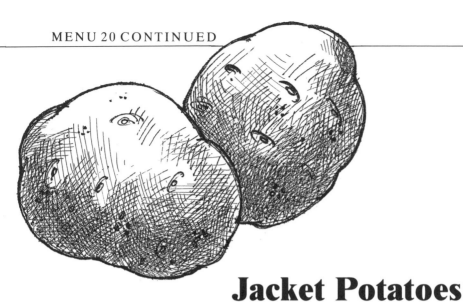

Jacket Potatoes

6 or more smallish-medium potatoes
oil
salt
butter or sour cream, chopped parsley for garnish

Baked potatoes can be microwaved but we prefer them baked in a conventional oven.

Scrub potatoes, then dry with a paper towel or similar. Prick the skins 2-3 times with a fork.
Lightly brush over with oil, then sprinkle sparingly with salt. This gives a most appealing texture to the potato skins.
Bake at 190°C for 1 hour. To serve, make a cross in the top and squeeze potato lightly. Garnish with butter or sour cream, sprinkled with chopped parsley.

Sweet Baked Parsnips

500g prepared parsnips
salt and freshly ground pepper to taste
1 tbsp margarine, melted
1 tbsp brown sugar

This recipe could be microwaved and crisped up under a grill.

Quarter the parsnips, then slice into serving size pieces. Blanch for approximately 6 minutes. Drain.
Place in a greased ovenproof dish, in a single layer.
Season. Pour over the butter, then sprinkle over the brown sugar.
Bake at 190°C for about 40 minutes, turning once during cooking.

Red Capsicum Salad with Snow Peas

2 large red capcisums, seeded and cut into thick strips (green
capsicums can used, but you then lose the lovely colour contrast)
2 cups snow peas

Dressing
½ cup olive oil
1 tbsp lemon juice
1 tbsp red wine vinegar
1 clove garlic, crushed
½ tsp dried basil or 2 tsp fresh chopped
½ tsp prepared or dry mustard
salt and freshly ground black pepper to taste

Place the capsicum strips into boiling water for 2 minutes,
until they soften. Remove and refresh under cold running water,
then drain well.
Blanch the whole snow peas in boiling water for just 30
seconds, then refresh immediately under cold running water.
Drain well.
Shake all the salad dressing ingredients together in a jar with a
lid.
Place the capsicum strips in the bottom of a serving bowl; now
arrange the snow peas so that they radiate out from a central
point in the middle of the dish, like the spokes of a wheel.
Pour over the well-combined dressing and serve (don't toss).

DESSERT

American Fudge Brownies
Page 143.

Mushroom Flan with Pumpkin-Rice Crust

Honey Glazed Carrots

Green Bean Salad with Mustard and Caper Vinaigrette

Chocolate Almond Torte

This flan is an impressive dish to serve to guests, both because of how good it tastes and because it's an attractively coloured dish with its orange crust, chocolate brown filling and creamy top. It makes a popular family meal and can also be served at room temperature, for a buffet or a special picnic perhaps.

*Boiled pumpkin takes on too much liquid, so that you risk a soggy crust.

**A 23 cm (9 inch) pie or flan dish may be used, but if so reduce rice to 1½ cups and pumpkin to ⅔ cup.

†The capsicum could be replaced by 1 cup sliced celery, courgettes, or very finely sliced leeks if desired.

††If the mushrooms have been sauteed then frozen, add them defrosted then drained to the frypan.

Don't skimp on the mushrooms for this dish — in the interests of both taste and eye appeal.

This recipe is not recommended for microwave or freezing.

Mushroom flan with Pumpkin-Rice Crust

Crust

2 cups cold cooked brown rice (preferably a day old)
1 tsp salt
2 tbsp sesame seeds
1 cup baked or microwaved pumpkin, mashed dry*
½ cup grated tasty cheddar cheese

Grease a 30 x 20 cm (12 x 8 inch) glass baking dish or similar.** Mix the crust ingredients until they are well combined. Press in the crust to line the bottom and sides, using your (wholemeal) floured hands.
Refrigerate if preparing ahead.

Filling

2 tbsp oil
2 medium onions, skinned and chopped
2 cloves garlic, crushed
2 capsicums, seeded and chopped†
350 g fresh sliced mushrooms††
3 eggs
1 cup cream, evaporated milk or sour cream
1 tsp mild prepared mustard
1 tsp Worcester sauce
1 tsp fresh chopped mint (optional)
1 tsp salt
freshly ground black pepper
½ tsp chilli sauce
1 cup tasty cheddar cheese, grated
1 sliced tomato

Heat the oil in a frypan and gently saute the garlic, onion and capsicum until soft. Add the fresh mushrooms and cook for a further 5 minutes. Lift the vegetables from the pan with a slotted spoon and drain again.
Beat the remaining ingredients together, except the cheese and the tomato.
Place the mushroom mixture into the pie crust, and top with the beaten egg/cream mixture.
Sprinkle the top with the cheese, then arrange the sliced tomato rings on top.
Bake at 190°C for 45 minutes or until set.

Honey Glazed Carrots

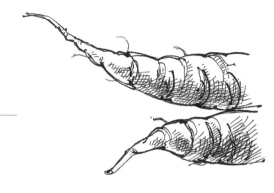

500 g young carrots
½ cup water
3 tbsp butter
⅓ cup honey
1 tsp salt
2 tbsp lemon juice
freshly ground pepper

Clean and scrape the carrots and cut lengthwise into medium strips. Put water and carrots in a pan with a lid and simmer for 8 minutes.
Add the butter, honey, salt and lemon juice.
Cook uncovered, stirring occasionally, until the water is evaporated and the carrots are just tender.
Reseason to taste and turn into a heated dish to serve.

This recipe may be microwaved.

Green Bean Salad with Mustard and Caper Vinaigrette

500 g green beans
2 tsp capers
1 tbsp lemon juice
1 tsp Dijon mustard
¼ cup olive oil

Place the prepared but uncut beans into a small amount of boiling water and cook for 5 minutes.
Drain, then refresh under running cold water and pat dry.
Mash the capers with a fork, add the lemon juice, seasoning and oil, then mix or shake thoroughly.
Pour over the cooked beans while they are still warm.
Refrigerate if you are preparing ahead, but serve at room temperature.

DESSERT

Chocolate Almond Torte
Page 146

Spanakopita

Stuffed Aubergines

Greek Salad

Baked Alaska with Fruit

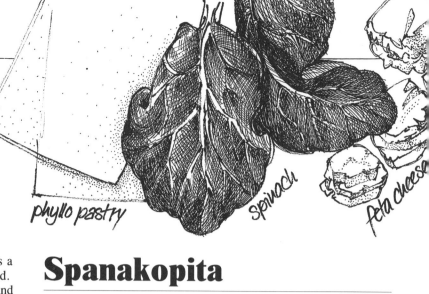

phyllo pastry spinach feta cheese

This famous spinach pie is a favourite all over the world. Made with phyllo pastry and feta cheese, it is distinctively Greek in origin, though we have added some touches of our own. It's complemented beautifully by stuffed aubergines and, of course, a Greek salad.

*Silverbeet may be substituted for spinach — 750 g silverbeet = 400 g destalked, deribbed prepared leaves

**Feta is the cheese more commonly used in Greek dishes such as Spanakopita, but some people just don't like feta cheese and you can't always get good tasting feta. It seems a shame that someone might miss out on this lovely dish for either of these reasons, so we've found that gruyere provides a very worthy alternative.

†There are 27 sheets of phyllo in one 375 g packet.

Spanakopita is not suitable for microwaving. It freezes well, though, when slightly underbaked. Reheat in a hot oven.

Spanakopita

400 g prepared spinach*
1 large onion, skinned and chopped finely
2 cloves garlic, crushed
2 tbsp oil
1 large grated carrot
2 tsp chopped fresh dill (optional) or ½ tsp crushed dill seeds
200 g feta cheese, crumbled or grated or gruyere**
250 g cottage cheese
6 eggs, beaten
¾ cup milk or cream
½ tsp chilli sauce
½ tsp prepared mustard such as Dijon
¾ cup sharp grated cheddar
1 tsp salt, or more to taste
freshly ground black pepper
18 sheets of phyllo pastry†

Wash the spinach leaves, shake dry and chop finely. Saute or microwave the onion and garlic in the oil until soft. Add the carrot and the spinach. Cook, covered, for about 6 minutes more (microwave for 3), shaking the pot regularly to prevent sticking. Drain well. Press as much excess liquid as possible from the spinach.
When cool, add the dill, the feta or gruyere and the cottage cheese.
Beat the eggs with the milk or cream, the chilli sauce and the mustard and add.
Mix in the cheddar, salt and some good grinds of black pepper. Check the seasonings at this point and adjust to your taste.
Pre-heat the oven to 190°C.
Unwrap the phyllo pastry and place between 2 dry tea towels.
Grease a 30 x 23 cm (12 x 9 inch) oven dish or similar. Place 2 sheets of phyllo pastry in the bottom of the pan, allowing any overlap to climb the sides.
Brush with melted butter, then add another 2 sheets.
Repeat the process until you have 10 layers.
Pour in the filling and spread it evenly over the pastry. Cover with another 8 sheets of phyllo, buttering between 2 and on top of the final sheet. Tuck any overlap down the sides.
Bake at 190°C for 45-50 minutes. (May be turned to 180°C after 20 minutes.)

Stuffed Aubergines

These also make a delicious base for a lighter meal, served with some bread and a salad.

3 small aubergines, each weighing 250-300 g, or 2 largish, 450-500 g each
1 medium onion, skinned and finely chopped
2 cloves garlic, crushed
3 tbsp margarine or butter
1 cup finely diced celery
3 medium tomatoes, diced finely
⅔ cup hot water
1 tsp instant onion or mushroom stock
½ cup currants
2 cups cooked brown rice
salt to taste
freshly ground black pepper
1 tsp nutmeg, freshly grated if possible
2 tsp lemon juice
½ cup roasted sunflower kernels (microwave 6 minutes, stirring every 2 minutes and season)
2 tbsp sour cream (optional)
½ cup finely chopped parsley for garnish

Slice the aubergines in half lengthwise. Carefully cut around the flesh in each half, leaving about 6mm (¼ inch) with the skin. Now scoop out the flesh with a teaspoon and dice it finely. Lightly salt the inside of the aubergine shells and invert them to drain.
Saute the onion and garlic in the butter, using a large frypan, until the onion is soft. Now add the celery, the aubergine flesh and the tomatoes. Saute briefly, stirring, then add the hot water with the stock dissolved in it. Simmer for about 5 minutes, then remove from the heat.
Add the rest of the ingredients except the lemon, sunflower kernels, sour cream and the parsley. Mix well. The mixture can be set aside at this stage if wished.
Ensure oven is pre-heated to 180°C.
Lastly, add the lemon juice, roasted kernels and sour cream (if used) and mix.
Dry the drained aubergine shells with kitchen paper and pile the filling into the shells.
Place in an oven dish and bake at 190°C for about 30 minutes, or until piping hot (or microwave this final stage).

This mixture may also be used to stuff capsicums. Simply cut the tops off 6 (8 if they're small) green or red capsicums, and remove the core and the seeds.
Place them in an ovenproof dish, fill with the stuffing then brush each one generously with oil.
Bake in a pre-heated oven at 190°C for 30-45 minutes.

This recipe freezes well. Reheat in a hot oven.

Greek Salad

1 medium-sized fresh lettuce, torn
2 large green peppers, seeded and cut into strips
100 g sliced feta cheese (optional)*
12 or so black olives
¾ cup bean sprouts
2 medium firm red tomatoes, cut in quarters or eighths
¼ cup basic vinaigrette

Toss altogether with the vinaigrette just before serving.

*The feta cheese is optional here because of its presence in the Spanakopita and also because the other 2 dishes in this menu are quite substantial.

DESSERT

Baked Alaska with Fruit
Page 147.

Indonesian Gado Gado Flan

Steamed Silverbeet

Courgette Combo

Fruit Compote

Indonesian Gado Gado Flan

This is a most unusual flan, stumbled upon in a moment of inspiration. The combination of ingredients may sound unlikely, but in fact they really do work. This dish, with its potato crust, always wins compliments.

*Before you start, please note that the crust is baked first, separately, so time must be allowed for this. It can, however, be baked, cooled and set aside or refrigerated until needed.

This flan is not suitable for microwaving. It freezes well — reheat from frozen in a 200°C oven until heated through.

Crust*

600 g potatoes (3-4 medium sized), peeled and grated
1 tsp salt
½ tsp ground cumin
¾ cup grated cheddar cheese, packed
freshly ground black pepper

Filling

3 medium-sized onions, peeled and sliced finely
4 medium-large firm ripe tomatoes, sliced
½ cup crunchy peanut butter
½ tsp salt
2 tsp brown sugar
3 tsp lemon juice
1 tsp fresh ginger, skinned and minced
1 tsp soya sauce
1 cup water
½-1 tsp sambal oelek or 1 tsp chilli sauce
¾ cup grated cheddar cheese (second measure)
1 egg
¾ cup sour cream
salt and pepper to taste
¼ cup pumpkin kernels

Sprinkle the grated potatoes with the 1 tsp of salt and leave to drain for about 15 minutes. Turn the oven to 190°C. Squeeze any water from the potatoes, mix in the seasonings, cumin and cheese, then press with floured hands (wholemeal) into the bottom and sides of a very well buttered 30 x 20 cm (12 x 8 inch) glass baking dish or similar.
Bake for 40-45 minutes at 190°C.
Saute or microwave the onions in a little butter until soft, then remove with a slotted spoon and set aside. Slice the tomatoes into rounds and set aside to drain.
Place the next 8 ingredients in a saucepan over a medium heat. Mix well and bring to the boil, stirring regularly. Simmer 5 minutes to thicken sufficiently, then set aside.
Spread the second measure of cheese into the baked crust, followed by the sauteed onions. Now layer in the sliced, drained tomatoes. Pour the gado gado sauce evenly over the tomatoes.
Lastly, beat the egg, sour cream and seasoning together and pour this over the top of the gado gado.
Sprinkle with the pumpkin kernels and bake for 35-40 minutes. Serve immediately.

Steamed Silverbeet

1 kg silverbeet
salt and freshly ground pepper to taste
2 tsp butter

Wash the beet, then remove most of the white stalks from
the leaves.
Chop the greens roughly and place in a large saucepan with the
seasonings (or microwave if you prefer).
Cover and cook on medium high, shaking the pot occasionally
to prevent sticking. The beet leaves steam in the water clinging
to them — this should take approximately 7 minutes. Stir in the
butter and serve immediately.

Silverbeet is at its best cooked
so simply and makes a perfect
accompaniment to a Gado
Gado flan.

Courgette Combo

500 g courgettes, sliced diagonally in a 2.5 cm (1 inch) chunks
½-1 red capsicum, seeded and sliced into long thin strips
2 tbsp sour cream
2 tbsp oil
1½ tbsp cider or white vinegar
½ tsp salt
freshly ground black pepper
1 chopped spring onion

Drop the courgettes into approximately 1½ cups of boiling
salted water for 2 minutes.
Remove and hold under cold running water until cool. Drain
then dry on kitchen paper. Now place in a serving bowl with
the red pepper strips, cover and refrigerate until ready to serve.
Blend the sour cream, oil, vinegar and seasonings vigorously
with a fork until well mixed, then add the spring onions. Mix
the dressing through the courgettes just before serving.

Use a mixture of green and
yellow courgettes for this
dish if you can get them
easily — it makes no
difference to the taste, but is
an attractive colour
combination.

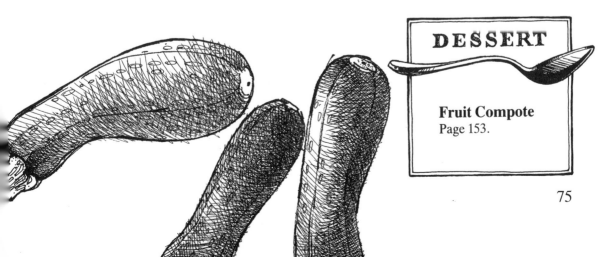

DESSERT

Fruit Compote
Page 153.

75

Leek, Tofu and
Tomato Flan

Broccoli with Toasted
Almonds and Lemon or
Hollandaise Sauce

Oven Crisped Potatoes

Pavlova

This flan is most attractive,
with its lattice topping, and it
tastes great, too.

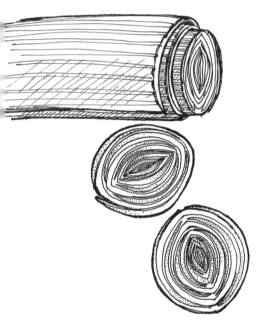

*If you are serving the flan
with the oven crisped
potatoes, you should place
the potato dish in the oven
about 30 minutes before the
flan in order to serve them
together.*

*This recipe is not
recommended for the
microwave, but it freezes well
if baked slightly underdone.
Wrap in foil and freeze. Thaw
before reheating in a 200°C
oven.*

Leek, Tofu and Tomato Flan

Pastry

1 cup wholemeal flour
1 cup plain flour
1 tsp salt
¼ cup parmesan cheese
125 g butter, cold
⅓ cup chilled water (approx.)

Place the flours, salt and cheese into a food processor bowl.
Cut the cold butter into 6 pieces and place on top of the dry
ingredients.
Process, using the pulse button, and at the same time add the
water through the feed tube. You may not need all the water —
the particles of dough should just begin to 'ball'.
Remove from the bowl, shape into a ball, cover with plastic
wrap and place in the refrigerator for half an hour if time
permits.
Butter a 30 x 20 cm (12 x 8 inch) shallow baking dish or similar
and line the bottom and sides of the dish with two thirds of the
pastry. Roll out the remaining third and cut into strips for the
lattice topping.

Filling

2 large leeks, sliced in 6 mm (¼ inch) slices (use most of green
part as well as white)
2 tbsp butter
2 firm ripe tomatoes, chopped
3 spring onions, finely chopped including green tops or 1 small
onion, very finely chopped
1 cup grated gruyere cheese
150 g firm tofu, sliced
4 eggs
1¼ cups milk
1 tsp Dijon mustard or similar
3 tbsp French onion soup mix
1 tbsp fresh oregano, chopped or 1 tsp dried
2 tbsp parsley, chopped
salt and pepper to taste

Melt the butter and saute (or microwave) the leeks in it until
soft. Allow to cool while you prepare the other ingredients.
Pre-heat oven to 200°C.
Place the leeks, chopped tomato, spring onion and sliced tofu
into the prepared baking dish. Sprinkle the cheese over the top.
Whisk all the remaining ingredients together, reserving a very
small amount of the egg mixture for glazing the top of the flan.
Arrange the reserved pastry strips on top of the filling in a
lattice work pattern, then brush the strips lightly with the
reserved egg mixture.
Bake at 200°C until the filling is set and the lattice pastry is
crisp, about 40 minutes. Lower heat to 180°C after 20 minutes
if the flan seems to be cooking too fast.

Broccoli with Toasted Almonds and Lemon or Hollandaise Sauce

600 g broccoli
60 g butter
3 tbsp lemon juice
salt and freshly ground black pepper
¼ cup flaked almonds, toasted*

Slice the broccoli into thin florets with plenty of stalk attached.
Place in a small amount of boiling, salted water and cook, covered, for 3-4 minutes over a medium high heat. Drain well.
In the same saucepan, melt the butter, then add the lemon juice and seasoning. Whisk to combine.
Gently toss the broccoli in the sauce.
Turn out onto a heated serving plate, sprinkle over the toasted almonds and serve immediately.

Toast the flaked almonds by placing in a heavy-based frypan. Heat, stirring, until the almonds begin to colour (or microwave on high 4 minutes, stirring once).

The lemon sauce is adequate for a more casual meal, but we recommend you make this dish using hollandaise sauce (p. 167) if you want to impress. Instead of tossing the broccoli in the sauce, pour the hollandaise over the broccoli immediately before serving, then garnish with the toasted almonds.

Oven Crisped Potatoes

These bite-sized morsels with their crispy coating are very quick and easy to prepare.

4 tbsp oil
2½ tbsp butter
1 kg potatoes, peeled and chopped into bite-sized pieces
1 cup wholemeal flour
1 tsp salt
¾ tsp paprika
¾ tsp freshly ground pepper
sprig of fresh parsley for garnish

Pre heat the oven to 200°C.
Place the oil and butter into a large shallow baking dish, at least 23 x 30 cm (9 x 12 inches).
Melt the oil and butter together in the oven as it heats.
Dry the potato chunks on kitchen paper or similar, then turn them in the melted butter/oil mixture.
Mix the flour, salt, paprika and pepper together. Now dredge the potato chunks in the flour mixture, so that each one is coated with the mixture.
Place the coated potato chunks into the baking dish — they should lie in a single layer, or the coating won't be crisp.
Bake at 200°C for about 1¼ hours, turning after 30 minutes.
For extra crispness, finish under a hot grill for 5 minutes, turning once.
Serve on a heated dish, garnished with a sprig of parsley.

DESSERT

Pavlova
Page 148.

Gazpacho Soup

Farmhouse Pie

Carrot Tabouleh

Crisp Green Salad

Cheater's Mocha Mousse

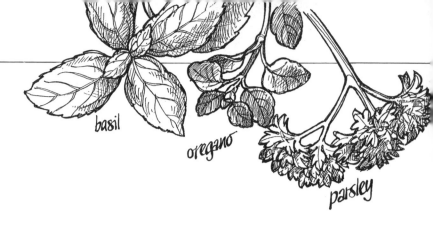

basil

oregano

parsley

This very quick, tasty, chilled soup can be prepared in minutes.

Gazpacho Soup

1 425 g tin whole tomatoes with juice
½ 420 g tin tomato juice
3 cloves garlic, crushed
1 medium cucumber, peeled, seeded and chopped roughly
2 capsicums, seeded and roughly chopped
1 large onion, peeled and quartered
½ cup good olive oil
1 slice wholemeal bread with crusts, cubed
2 tbsp red wine vinegar
1 tsp salt
½ tsp freshly ground black pepper
¼ tsp dried oregano or ½ tsp fresh chopped
¼ tsp dried basil or ½ tsp fresh chopped
½ tsp chilli sauce
½ tsp Worcester sauce
2 tbsp chopped fresh parsley

Place all the ingredients except the parsley into a food processor and process until very well blended.
Adjust the seasoning to taste.
If the soup seems too thick, add the remaining half tin of tomato juice.
Pour into a deep serving tureen and refrigerate until very well chilled.
Just before serving, stir the soup well and serve topped with the freshly chopped parsley.

This recipe is not suitable for freezing.

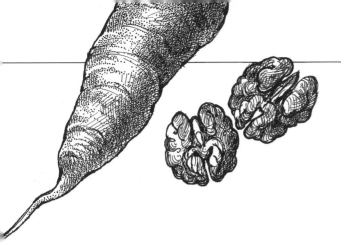

Carrot Tabouleh

½ cup kibbled wheat or burghul (bulghur)*
600 g carrots
2 spring onions, chopped
¼ cup parsley, chopped finely
1 tbsp chopped fresh mint or ¾ tsp dried
½ cup toasted walnuts, chopped or toasted almonds, left whole
½ tsp salt
½ tsp freshly ground black pepper
3 tbsp lemon juice
½ tsp chilli sauce, or to taste
⅓ cup mayonnaise, preferably home-made (see p. 166)
6-8 black olives, stoned

If using burghul, soak 20-30 minutes.

   Put the kibbled wheat to soak in cold water for 30-40 minutes. Drain, turn out onto kitchen paper and pat dry.
Chop the carrots roughly and place in a food processor bowl. Using the pulse button, chop until the carrots have a crumbly appearance — but don't puree them.
Turn out into a serving bowl.
Add the chopped spring onions, parsley, mint and the kibbled wheat.
The tabouleh may be prepared to this stage, then covered and left in a refrigerator until 1-2 hours before serving.
Add the chopped walnuts or whole almonds and mix in.
Mix the salt and pepper with the lemon juice and chilli sauce. Pour into the carrot mixture and toss.
Add the mayonnaise and mix well.
Garnish with the olives and refrigerate, covered, until ready to serve.

Farmhouse Pie next pages →

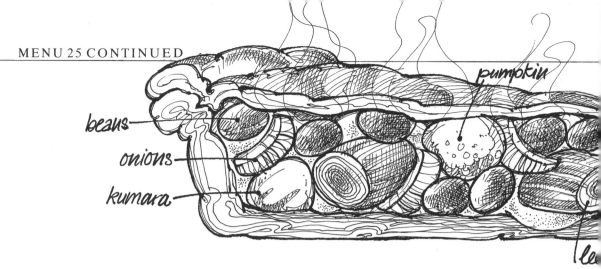

This pie makes a hearty meal which can be dressed up — or down — to suit the occasion, depending on what vegetables you choose to put in it. It's always popular.

Farmhouse Pie

Pastry

To line a 30 x 20 cm (12 x 8 inch) glass baking dish or similar, top and bottom.

1 cup wholemeal flour
1 cup rolled oats
½ tsp salt
125g cold margarine or butter
¾ cup water (approx.)

   Place the flour, rolled oats and salt into a bowl, then rub or cut in the margarine.
Mix with the very cold water and knead into a ball. Wrap in plastic and refrigerate while you prepare the filling.

Filling

1 kg of prepared vegetables — we suggest 600 g kumara, 2 onions, then 200 g pumpkin and 200 g leeks or courgettes
1 cup cooked dried beans, e.g. haricot, lima
1 quantity cheese and horseradish sauce

   Chop the vegetables into bite-sized chunks.
Place into boiling, salted water, in order of which takes longer to cook — use the list above as an example. You should have all the vegetables ready before you start, however, as kumara (or potato) will take only 4-5 minutes to par-cook from the time the water starts to boil. (Otherwise it will mush.)
Drain, reserving 1 cup of the stock for the sauce. Place the vegetables in a colander, then hold under cold running water for several minutes.

cheese and horseradish sauce

Cheese and Horseradish Sauce

75 g margarine or butter
½ cup flour
1 tsp salt and ½ tsp pepper
2 cups milk
½-1 cup reserved vegetable stock
2 tsp prepared horseradish sauce
125 g grated cheddar cheese

Melt margarine in saucepan, add flour and cook for 2 minutes. Remove from heat, add the milk in 2 lots, bringing to the boil between each addition. Add half a cup of the reserved vegetable stock and bring back to the boil.
Add the salt, pepper and horseradish, mix well, then add the cheese and check seasoning. Add some or all of the reserve stock if needed.

To Combine

Roll out the pastry to fit the baking dish bottom and sides, then the top. Mix the vegetables and the beans into the sauce, then pour the mixture into the pastry-lined dish and pinch down the top to the sides.
Brush the top with beaten egg and/or milk, make 3-4 slits for steam to escape and then bake at 200°C for 45-50 minutes.

The cheese and horseradish sauce may be microwaved. The pie can be frozen successfully if slightly underdone. Thaw before reheating.

Crisp Green Salad

This salad should be very simple — either crisp torn lettuce on its own, or a mixture of lettuce and spinach or silverbeet leaves, tossed with a mustard and garlic vinaigrette (see p. 165).

DESSERT

Cheater's Mocha Mousse
Page 140.

Gourmet Pumpkin and Zucchini Quiche

Adrienne's Asparagus Casserole

South Seas Salad

Italian Trifle Cake

This quiche looks most attractive when cut, revealing a creamy pumpkin filling resting on a thin layer of zucchini and a nutty pastry base.
The nuts used in the pastry do make this a more expensive quiche than most, but the filling ingredients are not expensive, and the end product is definitely superior.

It is perfectly possible to use the recipe for definitive pastry (p. 173) instead of the nut pastry given here; the alternative pastry is less substantial than the nut and has a different taste and texture, but is still very good. Use the larger measure of butter and omit the pre-baking part of this quiche recipe.

Gourmet Pumpkin and Zucchini Quiche

Nut Pastry

1¼ cups ground almonds or cashew nuts
½ cup wholemeal flour
½ cup plain flour
1 tbsp parmesan cheese
½ tsp salt
125 g butter, chilled
1 egg yolk

Place the nuts, flours, cheese and salt in a food processor.
Cut the butter into 6 pieces and place on top of the dry ingredients.
Process briefly, until the mixture resembles breadcrumbs. Add the egg yolk and process again, using the pulse button, just until the mixture begins to 'ball'.
Wrap in plastic wrap and refrigerate for 30 minutes if time allows.
Pre-heat the oven to 220°C.
Roll out to fit a greased 23 cm (9 inch) flan or quiche pan, preferably with a removable base (20 cm is too small).
Prick all over with a fork.
Bake at 220°C for 10 minutes, then allow to cool.

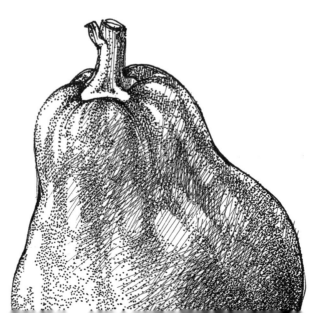

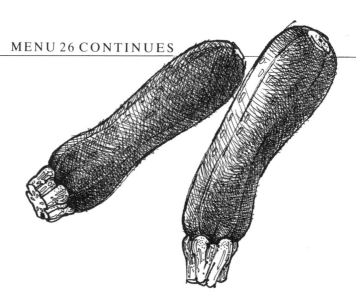

Filling

1 tbsp butter
1 large onion, finely chopped
450 g pumpkin, peeled and grated
½ tsp dried thyme
¼ tsp cinnamon
¼ tsp nutmeg
½ tsp paprika
1 tsp brown sugar
3 eggs
½ cup sour cream
1 tsp salt
1 tsp ground black pepper
1 tsp butter
2 medium zucchini, sliced into 6 mm (¼ inch) rings
1 cup grated cheddar cheese
2 tbsp finely chopped parsley as a garnish

Pre-heat the oven to 180°C.
Melt the butter in a pan over a gentle heat and saute the onion and pumpkin until tender (could be microwaved).
Place all the ingredients except the second measure of butter (1 tsp), the zucchini and cheese into a food processor or blender and process until smooth.
Melt the remaining 1 tsp butter and saute the zucchini rings for 2-3 minutes, until just tender.
Sprinkle ½ cup of the cheese into the cooled pastry base, then layer in the zucchini rings.
Pour in the pumpkin mixture, then sprinkle the top with the remaining ½ cup of cheese.*
Bake at 180°C for 40-45 minutes, or until the filling is set.
Sprinkle the parsley over the top of the quiche immediately before serving.

The filling rises very little during cooking, so the quiche case can be completely filled but shouldn't overflow.

This recipe is unsuitable for microwaving or freezing.

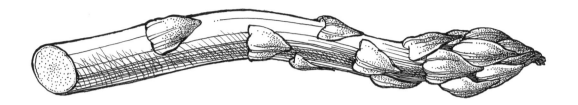

This simple recipe was contributed by a friend, Adrienne. It is superb and, if served on its own, makes a quick and easy supper or lunch.

Adrienne's Asparagus Casserole

1 340 g tin asparagus, cut into 5 cm (2 inch) lengths or the equivalent fresh steamed
1 420 g tin whole peeled tomatoes, drained and sliced or 5 medium fresh tomatoes, peeled and sliced
75 g butter or margarine
1 onion, peeled and finely sliced
250 g wholemeal bread, cut into small cubes
1 tsp salt
½ tsp freshly ground black pepper
2 tsp brown sugar
½ tsp dried basil or 1 tsp fresh chopped
1 tsp chopped fresh parsley

Pre-heat the oven to 180°C.
Generously butter a medium-sized casserole or souffle dish with a lid.
Lay the asparagus pieces into the casserole dish. Top with the tomatoes.
Melt the butter in a large fry pan and saute the onions until clear and soft.
Add the bread, salt, pepper, brown sugar, basil and parsley and stir for a few minutes.
Spread the bread mixture on top of the asparagus and tomatoes in the casserole and bake, covered, in the oven for 20 minutes at 180°C.
Remove the lid and bake a further 10 minutes to crisp the top.

The recipe could be microwaved to this stage.

South Seas Salad

⅓ medium-sized red cabbage, finely shredded
2 spring onions, chopped to include green leaves
3 tbsp toasted pumpkin kernels
1 crisp green apple, chopped unpeeled and sprinkled with 1 tbsp lemon juice
½ cup crushed pineapple, drained well
¼ medium lettuce
4 tbsp desiccated coconut, toasted

Dressing

1 cup sour cream
3 tbsp wine vinegar
2 tbsp chopped green capsicum
1 tbsp caster sugar
1 tsp salt
½ tsp freshly ground black pepper

Whisk or beat all dressing ingredients together until well combined. Mix all the salad ingredients together, except the lettuce and the coconut.
Mix with the dressing and chill, covered, for 30 minutes.
Serve on a bed of shredded lettuce, topped with the toasted coconut.

DESSERT

Italian Trifle Cake
Page 150.

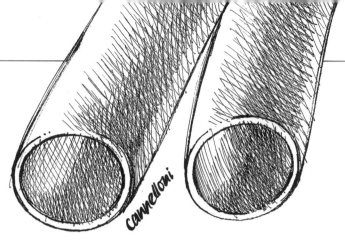

Pasta

Pasta is a wonderful vegetarian food, being infinitely versatile as well as nutritious and quick to prepare.

Types of Pasta

Cannelloni
Large tubes stuffed with various fillings and topped with sauce and cheese, then baked in the oven. Oven-ready varieties are available which need no pre-boiling.

Lasagne
Sheets of pasta, easy to make, but also available dry, fresh or oven-ready.

Macaroni
Usually in straight or 'elbow' lengths of hollow pasta.
Larger macaroni are called ZITI, and the largest, usually ribbed, is called RIGATONI.

Fettucine and Tagliatelle
These are ribbon-like pasta, available fresh or dry. They are often flavoured with spinach, herbs or tomato to make green or red noodles.

Spaghetti, Vermicelli and Spaghettini
These are all different thicknesses of long strands of pasta.

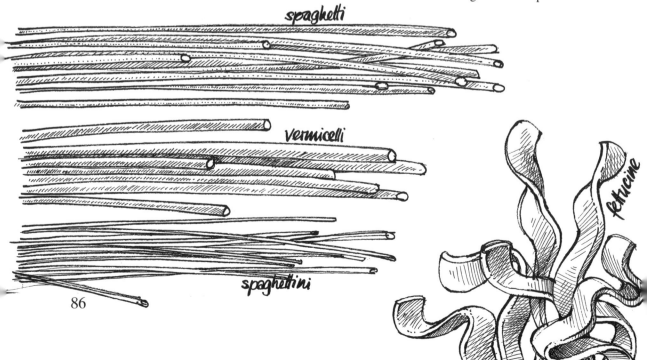

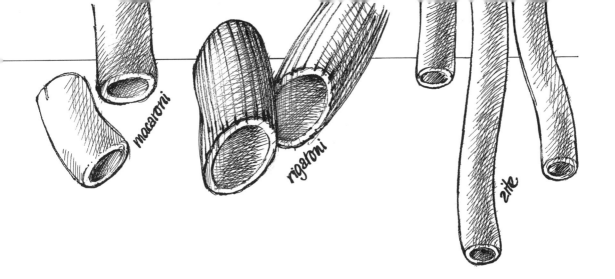

How to Cook Pasta

You do need a large saucepan, as the secret to successful pasta is to cook it in plenty of boiling water.
The proportion of water to pasta is 4 litres to 500 g pasta.

Bring the salted water to the boil, add the pasta, stir, then replace the lid to bring the water back to the boil as quickly as possible. Remove the lid and cook according to pasta type.

It is very important not to overcook pasta. It should be removed from the stove just as it reaches the 'al dente' stage, which is still firm but not hard. As soon as you think the pasta is slightly underdone, drain at once, as it does not stop cooking immediately.
As soon as the pasta is drained, dress it quickly, mix well and serve; or at least toss it with some butter or oil. Pasta left sitting without any dressing sticks, sags and droops — awful!

Fresh home-made pasta takes only 30 seconds to cook; fresh pasta sold in shops takes 2-2½ minutes.

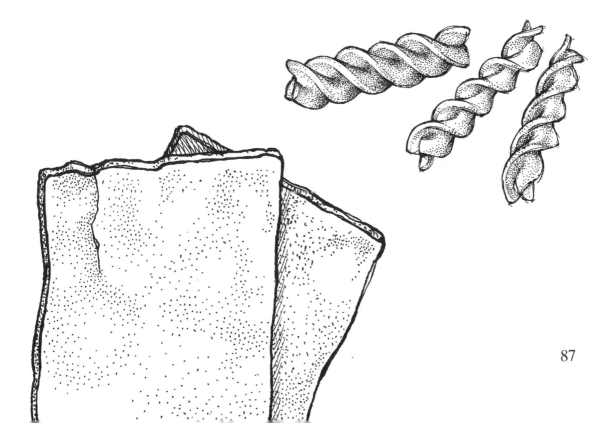

87

Making your own pasta is very simple if you have a food processor and a simple hand-operated pasta machine. The pasta machine isn't strictly necessary but is certainly worthwhile if you really like homemade pasta (we think it's vastly superior!).

Yes, we know, you just haven't time to make such quaint and homely products, but pasta can be refrigerated or frozen; *and* you can do so many different things with it; *and* you really only need a salad and French bread as accompaniments; *and* if you have pasta in the house, you've a meal in the house, even if you only toss it with butter, parmesan cheese and seasoning . . .

The following recipe makes about 550 g fresh pasta, enough for 4-6 hearty eaters.

Some pasta machines have a kneading attachment; if so, by all means use it instead.

Home-made Pasta

2½ cups plain flour
2 eggs
1 tsp salt
¼ cup water
1 tbsp olive oil

Place the flour, eggs and salt in food processor bowl with the metal blade. Mix the water and oil together.

Turn the machine on and pour the water/oil mixture in, all at once, while the machine is going. Just as the dough begins to 'ball', stop the machine and remove the dough.

Turn the dough onto a floured surface and knead for about 5 minutes until it loses its stickiness and gains an 'elastic' quality.*

Now — if you are using a pasta machine, use the dough immediately. If you plan to use a rolling pin, cover the dough and let it rest for 30 minutes. In both cases, the dough is cut into quarters before rolling.

Variations

To make wholemeal pasta, use 1 cup wholemeal flour to 1½ cups plain flour instead of 2½ cups plain.

Flavours

Use ¼ cup well-drained, cooked vegetables in the recipe instead of water, e.g. mashed carrot, mashed pumpkin, pureed spinach, or 2 tbsp pureed fresh herbs.

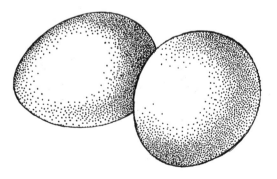

Pasta by Machine

Flatten quarter of the dough a little, then feed through the widest roller setting.

Fold the rolled dough into thirds and repeat the process 8 times, or until the dough is smooth and pliable, flouring both sides each time if it feels at all sticky.

When the dough is smooth and elastic, set the rollers one notch closer together and feed the dough through as before. Repeat this process, setting the rollers closer each time, until the dough is a long strip as thin as you want it.

Cut the strip in half crosswise for ease of handling, then place this on a floured surface while you roll the remaining portions. Leave the strips uncovered to dry for 5-10 minutes until it feels still soft but 'leathery'.

Each machine has cutting instructions, i.e. which attachment will produce fettucine, which tagliarini, etc. Lightly flour the cut noodles to keep the strands separate; pile the cut noodles loosely, or lay them in rows as you cut.

Pasta made with a machine is much faster than hand-made.

If you make more noodles than you need, dry them for 30 minutes-1 hour, then place in a plastic bag and refrigerate for up to 2 days or freeze for up to 2 months (don't thaw before cooking). If freezing, freeze in single, separate layers.

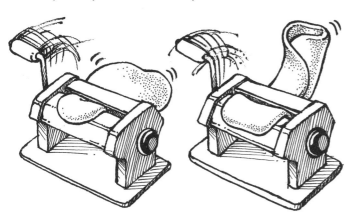

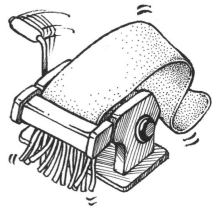

Pasta by Hand

Once the dough is turned out of the processor onto a floured board it should be kneaded for about 5 minutes, or until smooth and elastic. Then cover with plastic wrap and leave for 20-30 minutes.

Roll out quarter of the dough very thin, flouring both sides as needed. The dough should be about 1 mm ($\frac{1}{16}$ inch) thick, and shaped into a rectangle.

Lay the rolled dough on a floured surface and let it dry, uncovered, for 5-10 minutes.

On a floured surface, flour a strip of the rolled-out pasta, then roll up as you would a swiss roll.

Cut slices from it as wide as you want the noodles to be — e.g. fettucine is about 6 mm ($\frac{1}{4}$ inch wide), lasagne is about 6 cm wide (2 inches).

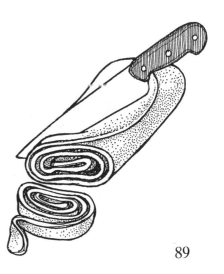

89

Spaghetti Napoli

Baked Rigatoni with Tomato and Mushrooms

Super Ice Cream and Fresh Fruit

Spaghetti Napoli is a basic and traditional Italian dish which is extremely simple to make.

Spaghetti Napoli

1 500 g packet spaghetti
2 large onions, skinned and finely chopped
3 cloves garlic, crushed
1 capsicum, finely chopped
2 tbsp olive oil
2 425 g tins tomatoes or 1 kg fresh tomatoes with skins removed
2 tsp tomato paste
1 tbsp chopped fresh basil or 1 tsp dried
1 tbsp chopped fresh oregano or 1 tsp dried
1 tsp brown sugar
1 tsp salt, or to taste
1 tsp freshly ground black pepper
3-4 drops of chilli sauce (optional)
grated parmesan cheese for serving

Serve with French bread and a simple green salad.

Saute (or microwave) onions, garlic and capsicum in the olive oil gently, until very soft.
Add the chopped tomatoes, tomato paste, herbs, sugar, salt, pepper and chilli sauce if you are using it.
Simmer very gently, uncovered, over a low heat for about 30 minutes, or until the sauce is reduced by approximately half.
Adjust the seasoning and serve over the cooked spaghetti, sprinkled with parmesan cheese.

This sauce microwaves and freezes well.

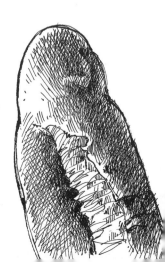

Baked Rigatoni with Tomato and Mushrooms

An excellent party dish, tasty but simple to prepare.

500 g rigatoni
250 g mushrooms
30 g butter
1 recipe of Napoli sauce (see opposite page)
1 425 ml tin tomato juice
2 cups grated mozzarella cheese
½ cup parmesan cheese, grated
125 g cottage or ricotta cheese
salt to taste
freshly ground black pepper (generous)

Start the rigatoni cooking according to instructions.
Saute the mushrooms in the butter for 5 minutes over a gentle heat.
Pre-heat the oven to 200°C.
Toss together the cooked rigatoni, the Napoli sauce, tomato juice, mushrooms, 1 cup of the mozzarella cheese, a quarter of a cup of the parmesan and the cottage or ricotta cheese.
Butter a 30 x 20 cm (12 x 8 inch) baking dish or similar, and pour in the rigatoni/sauce/cheese mixture.
Top with the remaining mozzarella and parmesan, then bake at 200°C for 20-30 minutes or until the cheese is melted, or microwave on medium high for 15 minutes.

Serve with French bread or a green salad.

This recipe freezes well. Reheat in a microwave or conventional oven.

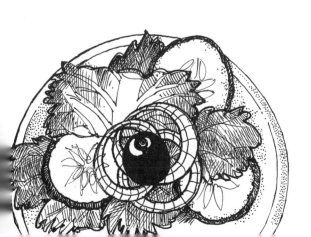

DESSERT

Super Ice Cream and Fresh Fruit
Page 138.

**Vegetable Lasagne
Verdi**

Fruit Flummery

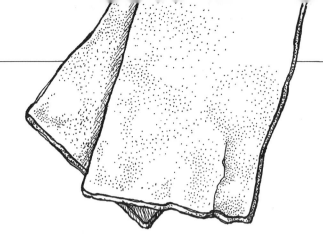

Lasagne is a wonderful dish
to serve to friends, as it's a
perfect complement to
company and conversation.
It's substantial and takes only
a minimum of time to
prepare, considering it's
really a meal on its own.

*Silverbeet may be
substituted for spinach — 400 g
of fresh beet, i.e. weighed
with most of white stalk
removed.*

Vegetable Lasagne Verdi

400 g par-cooked lasagne or 6 sheets of oven-ready lasagne
1 quantity of mushroom sauce (see the next page)
1 quantity of cheese sauce (see the next page)
250 g cooked spinach, or frozen (= 350 g fresh)*
1 250 g carton of cottage cheese
50 g cheddar cheese
3 tbsp parmesan cheese

Grease the bottom of a shallow oven dish and cover it with
lasagne strips, or with 2 sheets of oven-ready lasagne. An ideal
dish would measure 30 x 23 cm (12 x 9 inches) and be 6 cm
(2.5 inches) deep.

If you are using ordinary lasagne, pre-heat your oven to 180°C.
Spread half the mushroom sauce over the pasta, then cover this
with one-third of the cheese sauce.

Press any liquid from the cooked or thawed spinach. Spread half
of this spinach evenly over the cheese sauce and top with half the
carton of cottage cheese.

Repeat once more, then top with the remaining lasagne, spread
with the last third of the cheese sauce and sprinkle with the
grated cheddar and parmesan. If you are using the oven-ready
lasagne, let the dish stand for several hours to allow the pasta to
soften. Bake for approximately 45 minutes at 180°C or until the
top is a bubbling golden brown or microwave on medium high for
15 minutes.

Mushroom Sauce

1 onion, skinned and chopped
2-4 cloves garlic, crushed
150 g mushrooms, sliced*
2 tbsp oil
2 cups cooked dried beans, preferably soya, mashed
salt and pepper to taste
1 tsp oregano (dried), or 1 tbsp fresh chopped
1 tsp sugar
2 420 g cans of whole tomatoes or 1 kilo fresh, skinned

Variation
Use 400 g unpeeled, diced eggplant instead of the mushrooms. If using eggplant, increase the oil to 4 tbsp.

Saute the onion, garlic and mushrooms in oil until the onions soften. Add the remaining ingredients and simmer until the mixture is reduced and thickened.

Cheese Sauce

60 g butter
⅓ cup flour
salt, pepper and a pinch of nutmeg
2 cups milk
125 g cheddar or swiss cheese, grated (1 cup, packed)
3 tbsp parmesan cheese, grated

Lasagne needs only tossed green salad and perhaps a loaf of crispy French bread as an accompaniment.

Lasagne freezes well, either baked or unbaked. It can be reheated in a microwave or conventional oven until hot and bubbly.

Melt the butter in a saucepan, then add the flour, salt and pepper and nutmeg. Blend until smooth.
Gradually add the milk, stirring constantly until the sauce thickens. Stir in the cheeses.

DESSERT

Fruit Flummery
Page 155.

**Tagliatelle with
Primavera-Yoghurt
Sauce and Nuts**

**Fettucine with Spinach
and Walnut Sauce**

**Super Ice Cream and
Fresh Fruit**

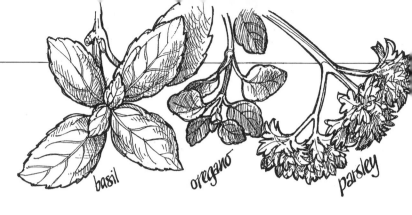

basil   oregano   parsley

This is a beautifully balanced
dish, in terms of both colour
and texture.

Tagliatelle with Primavera-Yoghurt Sauce and Nuts

500 g tagliatelle
45 g butter
1 medium onion, skinned and cut into thin slices
3 cloves garlic, crushed
1 red or green capsicum, cut into strips
1 cup (100 g) sliced fresh mushrooms
1 cup broccoli, cut into florets with a strip of stalk attached
1 medium zucchini, halved lengthwise and sliced
1 medium carrot, cut into julienne strips
¼ cup dry white wine or stock
1 tbsp chopped fresh basil or 1 tsp dried
1 tbsp chopped fresh oregano or 1 tsp dried
1 tsp honey
4 fresh tomatoes, skinned and chopped
1 tbsp chopped parsley
1 tsp salt
plenty of freshly ground black pepper
50 g almonds or cashew nuts, lightly toasted
½ cup plain yoghurt
¼ cup cream
½ cup grated parmesan cheese, plus extra for serving

*Other vegetables may be
substituted for those given in
the recipe — what you fancy
at the time of cooking, or
what's available.*

First, prepare your vegetables so that they don't lose their
crispness through overcooking as you proceed to each step.
Heat the butter gently, then add the onions, garlic and capsicum
and cook for 2 minutes.
Add the mushrooms, cook for a further 2 minutes. Then add the
broccoli, zucchini and carrot and cook for another 3 minutes or
until almost tender but still crisp. This should all be done over a
gentle heat.
The vegetables can be removed from the heat at this stage, and
set aside until you are ready for the meal and start the pasta
cooking.

*Serve with French bread and
a simple green salad.*

Add the white wine or stock, then the herbs, honey, tomatoes,
parsley, salt and plenty of freshly ground black pepper.
Toss in the cooked tagliatelle, the almonds, yoghurt, cream and
parmesan.

*This recipe is not suitable for
microwaving or freezing.*

Serve immediately, sprinkled with extra parsley and with a side
bowl of extra grated parmesan.

Fettucine with Spinach and Walnut Sauce

A deliciously different sauce complements this pasta. Do try to use olive oil rather than any other for this dish, though.

500 g plain fettucine
2 cups cooked spinach, finely chopped (400 g prepared leaves)*
30 g butter
2 tbsp olive oil
2 cloves garlic, crushed
1 cup chopped walnuts (not ground, but quite finely chopped.
Check that these are fresh)
½ cup cottage or ricotta cheese
1½-2 tsp salt
freshly ground pepper
2 tbsp toasted pine nuts, slivered almonds or pumpkin kernels

*Silverbeet can be substituted for the spinach.

Ensure that the spinach is drained very well to remove any excess liquid after cooking. (Cook 6 minutes, covered, with no extra water after washing — or microwave.)
Melt the butter and the oil together, and saute the garlic gently until it is cooked but not browned.
Set the pasta cooking.
Chop the walnuts.
Mash the cottage cheese with a fork, and place in a serving bowl, together with the butter, oil and garlic, salt and pepper.
Place the bowl in a warm oven and add the spinach and walnuts to it when the pasta is almost cooked.
Drain the cooked pasta, and immediately turn into the serving bowl. Toss thoroughly with the rest of the ingredients in the bowl.
Garnish with the toasted pine nuts, almonds or pumpkin kernels to serve.

Serve with French bread and a simple green salad.

This sauce is unsuitable for microwaving or freezing.

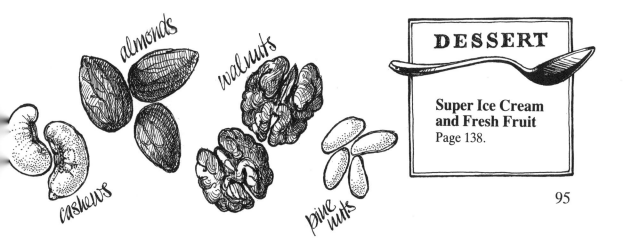

almonds

walnuts

cashews

pine nuts

DESSERT

Super Ice Cream and Fresh Fruit
Page 138.

95

Spinach Fettucine with
Mushroom Cream
Sauce

Macaroni Diablo

Super Ice Cream and
Fresh Fruit

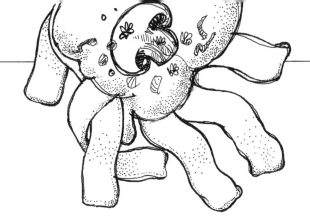

For the real success of this
recipe, try to use fresh herbs.
A simple green salad and
French bread are all that's
needed to complete this
menu.

Spinach Fettucine with Mushroom Cream Sauce

500 g spinach or herb fettucine
1 small onion, skinned and chopped very finely
1 large clove garlic, crushed
30 g butter or 2 tbsp margarine
500 g fresh mushrooms, sliced
1 tbsp wholemeal flour
2 cups cream
2 tsp chopped fresh basil or ½ tsp dried
1 tsp salt
lots of freshly ground pepper
1 tbsp grated parmesan cheese
1 tbsp sherry (optional)
1 tbsp chopped fresh parsley
1 finely diced tomato
¼ cup blue vein cheese, grated (optional)

Saute the onion and garlic in the butter until they are very
soft, then add the mushrooms and cook for about 5 minutes.
Stir in the flour, then slowly add the cream, stirring all the
time.
Simmer the sauce, stirring, for 15 minutes.
Add the herbs, seasoning, parmesan cheese and the sherry and
the blue vein cheese (if used).
Cook for another 2 minutes.
Cook the fettucine, toss with a little butter and then serve with
the mushroom sauce poured over the top, sprinkled with the
parsley and garnished with the diced fresh tomato.

This sauce is unsuitable for microwaving or freezing.

Macaroni Diablo

A very different way of serving macaroni to make an extremely tempting one-dish meal.
Add a salad and French bread if you wish.

400 g macaroni
2 large onions, chopped finely
2 cloves garlic, crushed
2 capsicums, green or red, chopped finely
2 small dried chillies, minced
2 tbsp oil
1 tbsp margarine or butter
1 tsp tumeric
3 tsp coriander
1 tsp of a good commercial curry powder
1 425 g tin whole tomatoes with juice or the equivalent weight of fresh, skinned tomatoes
2 tsp salt
lots of freshly ground pepper
1 tsp dried oregano or 1 tbsp fresh chopped
1 425 g tin whole kernel corn, drained
1 cup cooked kidney beans
2 cups plain yoghurt or 1 cup yoghurt and 1 cup sour cream
2 tsp runny or warmed honey
250 g (1 cup) cottage cheese or ricotta
1 tsp salt
2 cups grated cheddar cheese
1 cup grated mozzarella cheese
½ cup grated parmesan cheese

Take a large, heavy-based frypan. Saute the onions, garlic, capsicum and chillies in the heated oil and margarine until softened.
Stir in the turmeric, coriander and curry powder and saute for 1 minute.
Add the chopped tomatoes with their juice, the salt, pepper and the oregano.
Cook for 10 minutes over a gentle heat, stirring occasionally.
While the sauce is cooking, cook the macaroni till al dente.
Pre-heat oven to 180°C.
Toss the sauce together with the macaroni, the corn and the kidney beans. Check the seasoning.
In a bowl, mix together the yoghurt, honey, cottage or ricotta cheese and the salt. Add 1 cup of the cheddar, ½ cup of the mozzarella and ¼ cup of the parmesan.
Now take a large oval or round casserole and grease it.
Lay one-third of the macaroni mixture in the bottom, then one-third of the yoghurt mixture. Repeat this twice, ending with the last third of the yoghurt mix.
Top with the last 1 cup of cheddar mixed with the remaining ½ cup of mozzarella, and sprinkle with the last of the parmesan.
Bake, covered, at 180°C for 15 minutes. Remove the cover and bake for another 15-20 minutes, or until the top is bubbling and golden.

This recipe is unsuitable for microwaving or freezing.

DESSERT

Super Ice Cream and Fresh Fruit
Page 138.

Artichoke and Tofu Cannelloni

Butter Steamed Courgettes

Red Cabbage Salad

Baked Strawberry Shortcake

This cannelloni is truly luscious — a gourmet dish which is simple to assemble and relatively inexpensive in comparison with a gourmet meat dish. What more could you want for a special meal?

Because of the subtle flavour of the artichokes and tofu in this recipe, fresh herbs are to be recommended if possible. This recipe makes enough filling for 18 canelloni tubes. You can make your own pasta for this recipe.
This menu has the advantage that the cannelloni and the red cabbage salad can be prepared up to a day in advance. The only step to be done on the day of serving is to prepare and cook the courgettes. The courgettes and red cabbage salad add just the right touch of colour and texture contrast.

Artichoke and Tofu Cannelloni is suitable for freezing; just reheat in a microwave or a conventional oven.

Artichoke and Tofu Cannelloni

Filling

1 425 g tin artichoke hearts, drained well
125 g (½ block) tofu
2 tbsp butter
1 small onion, peeled and finely diced
2 large cloves garlic, crushed
1 tbsp lemon rind
juice of 1 lemon
1 tbsp chopped fresh basil or 1 tsp dried
1 tbsp chopped fresh oregano or 1 tsp dried
1 tsp Dijon mustard
1 tsp salt
1 tsp freshly ground pepper (measured!)
1 cup grated mozzarella cheese
½ cup cottage or ricotta cheese
½ cup grated parmesan cheese
½ cup cream
18 oven-ready cannelloni or 18 squares of home-made pasta (see p. 88).

Sauce

1 tbsp butter
1 small onion, peeled and chopped finely
2 cloves garlic, crushed
1 capsicum, seeded and chopped small
1 425 g tin tomatoes, undrained, or equivalent fresh, peeled
3 tbsp tomato paste

Topping

¾ cup cream
1 cup grated mozzarella cheese
½ cup grated parmesan cheese

Slice the well-drained artichokes into sixths.
Cut the tofu into small cubes.
Melt the butter in a heavy-based frypan and saute the onions and garlic gently until the onion is tender.
Add the artichoke pieces, the lemon juice, rind and the tofu. Saute for 2-3 minutes.
Add the basil, oregano, mustard, salt and pepper. Cook for another couple of minutes, then remove from the heat.
In a bowl, combine the mozzarella, the cottage or ricotta cheese, the parmesan and the cream.
Add to the artichoke mixture and mix well.
Using a teaspoon, fill the cannelloni shells with this mixture, pushing the filling down into the tubes with the spoon handle.
If you are using fresh pasta squares, fill and roll up as for crepes.
To make the sauce, melt the butter, saute the onion and garlic until soft. Add the capsicum, then the tomatoes and paste. Cook for 2-3 minutes.

Grease a 23 x 30 cm (9 x 12 inch) or similar baking dish. Layer 1 cup of the sauce into the bottom of the dish, then lay in the filled cannelloni, in a single layer.

Spread the remaining tomato sauce over the cannelloni, dot or pour over the cream. Then sprinkle first with the mozzarella, then with the parmesan.

If you are using oven-ready cannelloni, let the dish stand for at least 1 hour.

Bake in a pre-heated oven for 35-40 minutes, or microwave on medium high for 15 minutes or until bubbly.

Butter Steamed Courgettes

500 g courgettes, sliced in 6 mm (¼ inch) slices
½ cup water
1 tbsp butter
salt and freshly ground pepper to taste

Place the butter and water in a saucepan and bring to the boil.

Add the courgettes, cover and cook over a medium high heat for 5 minutes, shaking the pot to prevent sticking from time to time, or they are delicious microwaved for 2-3 minutes. (Cover and add the butter but not the water. Season.)

Red Cabbage Salad

350 g red cabbage
1 large green-skinned apple, chopped
1 large stalk celery, finely sliced
50 g raisins
50 g chopped walnuts

Dressing

3 tbsp sour cream or plain yoghurt
1 clove garlic, crushed
1 tbsp brown sugar
1 tsp wholegrain mustard
1 tsp salt
2 tbsp malt or tarragon vinegar
1 tbsp oil
freshly ground black pepper to taste

Shred the red cabbage and combine well with the apple, raisins and walnuts.

Mix the salad dressing together vigorously with a fork and stir into the cabbage mixture.

This salad improves with being made well in advance. Keep it covered in the refrigerator until it is needed.

DESSERT

Baked Strawberry Shortcake
Page 152.

Nancy's Baked Rishta and Aubergine

Pita Bread

Turkish Green Bean Salad

Apricot Flummery

This dish is based on a recipe contributed by a friend who grew up in Israel. Baked rishta and aubergine is simple to make, delicious and inexpensive — and its one of those dishes you miss when you haven't eaten it for a while.

*Broccoli may be substituted for eggplant — about 800 g. Don't salt the broccoli and blanch instead of saute.
If you are using significantly less eggplant than recommended, you may need to adjust the oil used for sauteeing accordingly.
Eggplants do absorb quite a lot of oil, although the salting does help to prevent this to some extent. It's best to use the minimum of oil, adding a little more to the pan as necessary — the eggplant does decrease in volume significantly as it cooks, and care should be taken to ensure that it does not taste oily.*

**Wholemeal or buckwheat noodles may be substituted if you wish.*

This recipe is suitable for freezing.

Nancy's Baked Rishta and Aubergine

2 medium eggplants, about 400 g each*
salt
⅓ cup oil, more if needed
4 hard-boiled eggs (optional)
1 large onion, finely chopped
2 tsp oil
425 g tin savoury tomatoes or 425 g tin tomatoes and juice or 500 g fresh tomatoes, skinned
3 tbsp tomato paste
2 tsp fresh oregano, chopped or ½ tsp dried
2 tsp fresh basil, or ½ tsp dried
1 small tsp salt
grinds of pepper
250 g thin egg noodles (or spaghetti)**
1 tsp oil
1 small onion, skinned and finely chopped
1 rib celery, diced finely (optional)
1 cup fresh wholemeal breadcrumbs or wheatgerm
2 tbsp butter or margarine

Slice the unpeeled eggplants into 1.25 cm (½ inch) slices, sprinkle lightly with salt on both sides and leave to drain for 30 minutes. Pat dry, then cut into walnut-sized pieces. Saute in the oil until the eggplant is turning lightly golden and the oil has been absorbed.
Hard boil the eggs if using and set aside. Peel and chop when cool.
Prepare a sauce by microwaving or sauteeing the onion in the oil until soft, then adding the tomatoes, tomato paste, herbs and seasonings. Mix well. (If you're using fresh tomatoes, cook until soft then add the rest of the ingredients.)
Now bring salted water to a boil. As you drop the noodles into the boiling water, break them into roughly 4-5 cm (2 inch) lengths.
Cook them till al dente, refresh under cold water and drain well.
Toss with the teaspoonful of oil.
Lastly, microwave or saute the small onion and the celery in the margarine or butter. Remove from the heat, add the breadcrumbs or wheatgerm and toss until well mixed.
Heat the oven to 180°C.
To assemble, butter a 30 x 20 cm (12 x 8 inch) baking dish.
Place a layer of eggplant in the bottom, then a layer of noodles. Follow this with the eggs (if used) and then the sauce. Finally, sprinkle over the breadcrumb topping.
Bake at 180°C for 30 minutes or until the dish is piping hot and the topping golden and crunchy (or microwave on medium high for 15 minutes, crisping the top under a hot grill.)

Pita Bread

2 cups plain flour
1 cup wholemeal flour
3 tsp salt
4 tsp of a dry fast acting yeast such as Surebake or 2 raised tsp of ordinary granulated yeast
1¼-1½ cups warm (slightly above blood heat) water
1 tbsp oil

Place the flours, salt and yeast into a bowl. Make a well in the centre and pour in the water with the oil added to it. Mix to a firmish dough.

Sprinkle some plain flour onto a board and knead the dough on this until it is smooth and elastic. This should take about 10 minutes.

Place the dough back in the bowl, cover and leave in a warm place for 30-40 minutes if you have time. This step may be omitted, but we advise including it if possible.

Divide the dough into 8 equal pieces, then knead each lightly before rolling out into a 15-17 cm (6-7 inch) round.

Place the rounds onto floured oven trays (4 to a tray) and leave in a warm place for 40-45 minutes until lightly puffed on top. Pre-heat the oven to 190°C.

Bake the rounds for 12-15 minutes, turning over with a spatula once during cooking.

Pita bread is traditionally served with Tabouleh (p. 49) or Hummus (p. 160), but it also complements the dishes in this menu superbly well. Making pita bread does take time, although you can do lots of other things as well as attending to it. Bread making should rarely be attempted when you're in a hurry, as you're unlikely to enjoy the process. So, if you need it quickly our advice is to buy it.

Pita bread may be frozen. Reheat from frozen in a hot oven.

Turkish Green Bean Salad

Delicious!

1 large onion, peeled and finely chopped
4 small dried chillies, minced
½ cup oil, preferably olive
2 tsp honey
2 large tomatoes, chopped
600 g fresh green beans, French cut (on a diagonal)
1½ tsp salt
freshly ground black pepper
chopped parsley
lemon juice to taste

Saute the onion and chillies in the oil until soft. Add the tomatoes, the honey and the beans, then the seasoning. Cover and simmer gently for 5-7 minutes, stirring occasionally. Remove from the heat and cool.

Serve at room temperature sprinkled with the parsley and a little lemon juice.

Plain crisp lettuce leaves may be added to this menu if desired.

DESSERT

Apricot Flummery
Page 155.

Sichuan Eggdrop Soup

Oriental Tofu and Vegetables in Ginger Sesame Seed Sauce

Cantonese Salad

Sue's Very Special Baked Cheesecake

This soup tastes so good it's hard to believe it takes so little time to prepare.

Sichuan Eggdrop Soup

4 cups vegetable stock, home-made or 4 cups water plus 3 tsp green herb instant stock
2 tsp cornflour
2 tsp soya sauce
½ cup corn, scraped fresh from a cob or tinned whole kernel or cream style
½ cup raw mushrooms, sliced thinly
¼ tsp ground white pepper
¼ tsp chilli sauce
salt and pepper to taste
2 eggs, beaten
1 tsp oil
1 spring onion, sliced finely

Place the stock in a large saucepan, reserving 1 tbsp of it. Mix this 1 tbsp with the 2 tsp cornflour and set aside. Heat the stock, adding the soya sauce, corn, mushrooms, white pepper and the chilli sauce.
Bring the stock to boiling point, then stir in the mixed stock/cornflour mixture to thicken slightly. Check the seasoning and adjust if necessary.
Beat the eggs and oil together lightly. Pour into a serving bowl or tureen.
Now pour the hot stock mixture over the beaten eggs in the serving dish, to cover the entire surface of the eggs.
Stir gently, then garnish with the spring onion and serve at once.

This soup is unsuitable for microwaving or freezing.

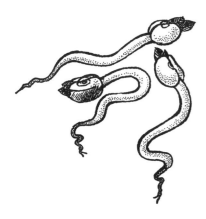

Cantonese Salad

400-450 g prepared spinach
150 g mung bean sprouts
2 cups thin Chinese noodles, cooked till al dente then drained well and cooled
Oriental dressing (p. 165)
individual onion rings (preferably red onion)
¾ cup roasted, salted peanuts.

Tear spinach leaves and place in a serving bowl. Mix in the bean sprouts and the cooked, cooled noodles.
Toss with the Oriental Dressing (see p. 165) immediately before serving and garnish with the onion rings and roasted peanuts.

Oriental Tofu and Vegetables in Ginger Sesame Seed Sauce

500 g firm tofu, cut in 1.25 cm (½ inch) cubes
¼ cup soya sauce
½ cup water
2 tbsp cornflour

Place the tofu cubes in the bottom of a shallow baking dish, in a single layer. Mix the rest of the above ingredients together, pour over the tofu cubes. Stir gently to coat the tofu with marinade.
Marinate, covered and chilled, for at least 1 hour and up to 24 hours. Stir occasionally.
Drain, but reserve the marinade.

½ cup sesame seeds, toasted*
6 tbsp oil
2 tsp fresh ginger, skinned and minced
3-4 small dried chillies, minced
2 medium carrots, cut into matchsticks
500g courgettes, cut into matchsticks
2½ cups broccoli florets, sliced thin and in 2 cm (¾ inch) lengths
1 tsp salt or to taste (optional)
2 tbsp medium sherry (optional)
¾ cup water

Heat 4 tbsp of the oil to medium high in a large frypan. Saute the marinaded tofu, turning, for 1-2 minutes or until it is golden. Remove with a slotted spoon and keep warm.
Add the last 2 tbsp of oil to the pan. Saute the ginger and chilli gently, then add the carrot sticks. Stir for a few seconds, then add the courgettes and the broccoli. Cook, stirring, for about 3 minutes.
Now add the sherry (if used), the reserved marinade and the water. Bring to the boil, then mix in the toasted sesame seeds and the tofu. Check seasoning and add salt if you wish.
Transfer the mixture to a heated serving dish.

This is a recipe everyone will enjoy, even if they haven't tried tofu before. The combination of nutty sesame seeds, tofu and ginger glazed vegetables is superb.

The secret to successful Chinese cooking is to have everything prepared ahead, as the actual cooking time is so brief. This makes good sense in any case, when you're having guests and ensures that you don't end up with pallid, tasteless vegetables because of overcooking — there's nothing worse! Prepare the vegetables, cover and refrigerate until needed.

The vegetables can be varied, e.g. the broccoli can be replaced by sliced celery or cauliflower, but do keep the carrot sticks and don't change the proportion of fresh ginger or sesame seeds.

*Toast sesame seeds in a dry pan over a gentle heat, stirring, until they turn golden or microwave approx. 4 minutes stirring twice.

This dish should be served with plain rice, and for this menu we recommend white rice as being more appropriate, in respect of both taste and colour.

This recipe is unsuitable for microwaving or freezing.

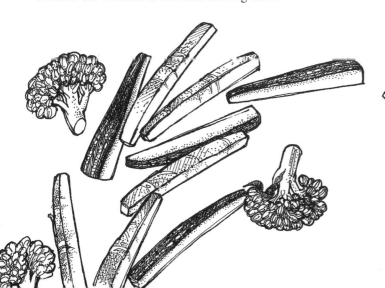

DESSERT

Sue's Very Special Baked Cheesecake
Page 154.

103

Chinese Egg Rolls with Sweet and Sour Sauce

Mandarin Braised Cauliflower and Nuts in Black Bean Sauce

Ginger and Lemon Cheesecake

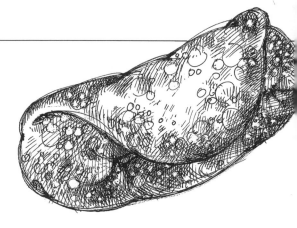

These egg rolls are quite wonderful, with their crunchy wrappings and delicious filling. Store-bought spring roll wrappers may be used instead of the oriental pancakes we use, but these are no more difficult to produce than crepes — just follow the recipe, it works well. The mixture should make approximately 16 pancakes.

Serve them accompanied by a bowl of sweet and sour sauce. The sauce can either be poured over the rolls, or used as a dipping sauce. (Small individual dipping saucers are ideal here if you have them.)
Serve the rolls on top of plain steamed rice or noodles.

Chinese Egg Rolls with Sweet and Sour Sauce

1 egg
1 tsp sugar
2 cups flour
2 tbsp cornflour
1 tsp salt
3 cups water

Place all the ingredients into a food processor bowl (metal blade) and blend for about 30 seconds, just until well mixed. This will produce a thin batter.
Pour into a jug for ease of handling.
Heat a 20 cm (8 inch) omelette or crepe pan.
Grease with oil or butter.
Pour in enough batter to cover the bottom of the pan thinly when 'swirled' over. Loosen the edges and turn over when bubbles appear on the surface. Cook the other side. The pancakes should be as thin as possible. Stack on top of each other, then allow to cool completely before filling. Wrap them in plastic wrap and refrigerate if you are preparing well ahead. Reserve 2-3 tbsp of the batter for sealing the filled rolls.

Filling

2 tbsp oil
1 onion, peeled and chopped very finely
2.5 cm piece of fresh ginger, peeled and minced
1 cup bean sprouts
200 g finely diced or chopped mixed vegetables*
½ cup finely diced or chopped celery
⅓ cup finely diced or chopped carrot
⅓ cup chopped mushrooms
2 tsp soya sauce
salt and freshly ground pepper to taste

*It's best to do this by hand. It makes about 1½ cups — use cauliflower, courgettes, capsicum, broccoli, etc.

Heat the oil in a pan and saute the onion and ginger until soft.

Add all the other vegetables and saute for 5-6 minutes. Stir in the soya sauce and seasonings, adjust if needed, then drain off any excess liquid. Allow to cool a little if time permits.

Take one pancake and place 2 tbsp of the filling mixture across the bottom of the end nearest you. Leave a 1.5 cm (½ inch) gap at each side. Bear in mind that they will resemble a (large) cigar shape when complete.

Roll over twice, then tuck in the side edges. Continue rolling up. Seal with the leftover batter, or beaten egg if you run out. Place the rolls seam side down on a dish.

Deep fry in hot oil until golden brown — this should take only a few minutes and they can be fried 2 at a time.

Drain on absorbent paper and keep the first ones hot in an oven until they are all cooked.

Serve immediately.

These rolls can be cooked, drained, then reheated in a hot oven later if you don't want to be rushed at the time of serving. (They are best served immediately, but still very good reheated.)

Egg rolls should not be microwaved, but can be frozen after being fried and cooled. Reheat from frozen in a hot oven.

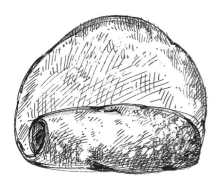

Sweet and Sour Sauce

1 tbsp vegetable oil
2 cloves garlic, crushed
1 tsp fresh ginger, skinned and grated or minced
1 small capsicum, seeded and sliced into strips
1 small dried chilli, chopped finely
2 tbsp malt vinegar
1½ tbsp brown sugar
1½ tbsp cornflour
1 cup vegetable stock or water
1 tbsp tomato sauce
¾ tsp salt or to taste
freshly ground black pepper

Heat the oil in a small saucepan, then saute the garlic, ginger, capsicum and chilli gently for 2 minutes.
Add the vinegar and brown sugar, and the cornflour mixed with the stock or water.
Stir in the tomato sauce, then the seasonings — adjust if needed.
Bring to the boil, stirring.
Reheat immediately before serving.

ginger

Mandarin Braised Cauliflower and Nuts in Black Bean Sauce

Prepare the vegetables, cook the noodles and soak the beans for this dish before you begin — then you can enjoy the cooking!

2 tbsp oil, preferably sesame or peanut
1 large onion, peeled, cut lengthwise and cut into thin slices
2 cloves garlic, crushed
1½ tsp peeled and grated fresh ginger
250 g cauliflower, thick stalk removed — break or cut into finger width florets
100 g green beans, cut lengthwise into strips
1½ cups vegetable stock or water
150 g silverbeet, weighed after removing stalks, washed and shredded
1 tsp honey
2 tbsp soya sauce
1½ tbsp black bean sauce or soaked and mashed fermented black beans
1 tsp freshly ground black pepper
1 tsp salt — taste before adding
1 tsp sherry (optional)
1 cup mungbean sprouts
1 cup thin egg noodles or spaghetti, cooked al dente
4 tsp cornflour, mixed with 2 tbsp water
½ cup whole raw cashews or walnut halves

This recipe could be microwaved, but we feel it is easier and quicker to cook on the stove.
It is unsuitable for freezing.

   Heat the oil in a large frypan or wok. Stir fry the onion, garlic, ginger, and the cauliflower for 4 minutes. Do not allow the onion to brown. Add the green beans and cook 2 more minutes.
Stir in the water or stock, silverbeet, honey, soya sauce, black bean sauce, pepper, salt and sherry. Simmer gently for 5 minutes.
Stir in the mung bean sprouts, noodles and the dissolved cornflour. Heat through gently until the sauce is slightly thickened and translucent. Stir in the nuts and serve immediately.

DESSERT

Ginger and Lemon Cheesecake
Page 157.

**Vegetable Tempura
with Dipping Sauce**

**Oriental Green Bean
Salad**

**Japanese Rice and
Peas**

Orange Sorbet

Most people (i.e. from 2 feet high up) find these irresistible. Almost any vegetable can be used, although kumara, potato and mushroom caps seem to be the most popular, along with aubergine, onion rings and cauliflower.

If you are cooking tempura for guests, it is wise to par-cook the battered vegetables before your guests arrive. Set aside on some kitchen paper until you are ready for the final cooking. This saves time and ensures that the batter will stay crisp for longer.

This recipe makes sufficient to coat approximately 3 cups prepared vegetables, enough for 4-6 people.

If you are refrying, the battered vegetables should be fried the first time only until they are barely coloured.

You don't need many pieces of tempura per serving, as the batter is quite filling.

Tempura is unsuitable to microwave or freeze.

Vegetable Tempura with Dipping Sauce

Slice the vegetables to be used into 1.25 cm (½ inch) slices where applicable; halve mushroom caps, cut capsicum and eggplant into 2.5 cm (1 inch) chunks.

Par-cook slices of each of the root vegetables in turn in a small amount of salted, boiling water. (Potato and kumara take longest at 4 minutes, carrot takes 3.) The other vegetables don't require pre-cooking.

Remove and cool under cold running water for a minute or two, then drain and dry thoroughly with kitchen paper.

Batter

1½ cups sifted flour
½ tsp of salt
1 tsp freshly ground black pepper
½ tsp curry powder
½ tsp five spice powder
1¼ cups water or beer
1¼ tsp prepared mustard
1 tbsp soya sauce
2 egg whites, stiffly beaten

Sift the flour, salt, pepper, curry and five spice powder into a bowl.

Mix in the water or beer, the mustard and the soya sauce. (The beer should not be flat.)

Lastly, fold in the stiffly beaten egg whites. Allow to stand for 30 minutes while you prepare the vegetables.

Place enough oil in a saucepan to half fill it. The saucepan should be fitted with a frying basket.

Now heat the oil to very hot, but not smoking. A bread cube should float to the top, golden (not black). Don't try to fry too much at one time, as this will lower the temperature so the batter will not seal, and the vegetables will be limp and soggy.

Drain on kitchen or absorbent paper. These can now be left for some hours if you are preparing ahead. Refry a second time just before serving.

Serve immediately on hot plates.

Dipping Sauce

½ cup dry sherry
½ cup soya sauce
2 tsp runny or melted honey
1 tbsp minced fresh ginger
and/or lemon wedges
or tomato sauce, preferably home-made
or satay sauce (see the recipe for satay sauce with the Indonesian Gado Gado Flan, p. 74).

Oriental Green Bean Salad

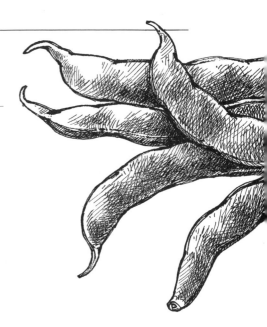

500 g green beans, prepared but left whole

Dressing

1 tsp juice from squeezed grated ginger (or press peeled sliced ginger through a garlic press)
1½ tsp honey
1½ tbsp soya sauce
1 tsp lemon juice
1 tsp sesame seeds, either raw or toasted

Boil or steam the green beans for 4-5 minutes — they should still be crisp.
Rinse under cold water and drain well.
Shake all the dressing ingredients together in a jar until well combined.
Toss the beans in the dressing, then sprinkle the sesame seeds over the beans just before serving.
Serve at room temperature.

Japanese Rice and Peas

4 cups cooked brown rice, very well drained, preferably cooked the day before
20 snow peas (or 2 cups frozen peas)
1 tbsp cooking oil

Seasoning

3¼ tbsp white vinegar
1 tbsp caster sugar
1 tsp salt
4 tsp preserved ginger, very finely diced
2 tbsp soya sauce
1 tbsp finely chopped spring onions or chives

Mix together the seasoning ingredients.
Cut the tops and bottoms from the snow peas and steam or boil lightly for 4-5 minutes. If you are using frozen peas, cook for 2 minutes only.
Cut the cooked snow peas into thin strips.
Heat the oil in a large frypan or wok.
Mix the rice and the seasoning mix together and fry over a medium high heat for about 3 minutes.
Serve garnished with the snow peas or peas and the spring onions or chives.

DESSERT

Orange Sorbet
Page 139.

Vegetable Tarkari

**Cucumber and
Capsicum Raita**

Baked Rice Pulao

**Mary's Chocolate
Coffee Pie**

Vegetable Tarkari

This quick and easy dish can
be prepared and placed on
the table in about 40 minutes
if required. It's based on a
Bangladeshi recipe, but we
have added a touch of
Malaysia with the coconut
cream, peanut butter and soya
sauce. These may be omitted
and the coconut cream
replaced with water; it's
delicious either way.
Serve Tarkari simply with
plain yoghurt (or the raita
given here) and brown rice if
you're in a hurry.
Serve with the Baked Rice
Pulao, adding puris or
chapatis (p. 161), a sambal or
two (p. 162-163 and p. 113,
115) and a salad if you can
afford more leisurely
planning.

*The eggplant does not require
salting for this recipe.*

*Tarkari may be microwaved
and it freezes well for up to 1
month.*

6 tbsp oil
2 medium onions, skinned and sliced thinly
3 large cloves garlic, crushed
4-7 small dried chillies, minced
1 tsp tumeric
2 tbsp coriander
1 tsp ground ginger
1 tbsp poppy seeds
2 medium potatoes, peeled and diced
1¼ cups water
1 medium-large eggplant, diced, unpeeled (500-600 g)*
1 tsp ground black pepper
2 tsp salt
4 medium tomatoes, chopped
300 g cauliflorets, sliced
1 cup diced courgette, celery, capsicum or a mix
2 tbsp peanut butter
1 tbsp soya sauce
1 420 ml tin coconut cream
2 tbsp pumpkin kernels

Heat the oil in a large, heavy-based frypan (or electric
frypan). Saute the onions, garlic and chillies together for a few
minutes, then add the tumeric, coriander, ginger and poppy
seeds. Saute gently for several minutes.
Add the potatoes, mix and saute for a few minutes. Then add
the water and the eggplant, followed by the pepper and the salt.
Cover and cook gently, stirring occasionally, for 15 minutes.
Now add the tomatoes, the cauliflorets and the courgette or
whatever you are using.
Stir in the peanut butter and the soya sauce.
Add the coconut cream and mix well.
Cover and simmer for another 15 minutes. Serve garnished with
the pumpkin kernels.

pumpkin kernels

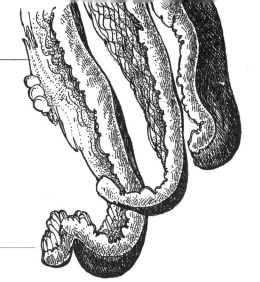

Cucumber and Capsicum Raita

2 small-medium cucumbers, peeled, seeded and sliced
1 tsp salt
1 red or green capsicum, seeded and sliced
½ cup natural yoghurt

   Sprinkle the cucumber slices with salt, then leave to drain in a colander for 20 minutes.
Drain and dry with a kitchen towel.
Combine the cucumbers, capsicum and yoghurt together in a serving bowl and serve.

Baked Rice Pulao

This is wonderful — but very simple.

This recipe can be frozen.

2 cups cooked brown rice
1 banana, sliced
1 cup cooked mixed vegetables, chopped or diced — carrots, peas, beans, celery, etc.
½ cup sliced, cooked mushrooms
70 g walnuts, roughly chopped
½ cup pumpkin kernels
½ cup cottage cheese
½ cup grated tasty cheese
½ cup currants
3 tbsp chopped parsley
2 tsp chopped fresh mint or ½ tsp dried
1 cup hot vegetable stock or 1 cup hot water plus 1 tsp green herb instant stock
2 tsp curry powder
1½ tsp salt
1 tsp freshly ground black pepper
½ tsp prepared mustard
¼ tsp nutmeg
½ tsp cinnamon
125 g sour cream or yoghurt

   Pre-heat the oven to 180°C.
Combine the rice with all the remaining ingredients except the sour cream. Mix well and check the seasonings.
Place into a 2 litre (3½ pint) round or square casserole dish, then spread the sour cream on top.
Bake for 35-45 minutes at 180°C or microwave on high 8-10 minutes.

DESSERT

Mary's Chocolate Coffee and Cream Pie
Page 131.

Potato and Green Pea Curry

Nutty Carrot Loaf

Celery and Apple Sambal

Plum or Prune Raita

Apricot Crepes

Potato and Green Pea Curry

It's easy to understand why the combination of potatoes and peas is a traditional favourite in curry-eating countries. This adaptation tastes delicious, and is simple to make.

Serve with plain steamed rice, puris (p. 161) and a green salad if desired.

Older potatoes are best. They can either be peeled, diced and cooked in boiling salted water for about 5 minutes and then held under cold running water and drained, or they can be diced and microwaved until just tender.

**Tamarind has a slightly sourish taste, but gains in flavour when cooked and is delicious in curries. It's usually packaged in a block as a very thick paste. It's well worth making an effort to get some if you're not familiar with it.*

This curry, when cooked so that not much liquid remains, can be used as a filling for samosas. See p. 159.

This recipe is suitable to freeze for up to 1 month.

4 tbsp oil
1 tsp poppy seeds
1 tsp mustard seeds
2 medium onions, skinned and chopped finely
5 cloves garlic, crushed
2 tsp cumin
2 tsp tumeric
4 tsp coriander
1 tsp ground black pepper
4-6 small dried chillies, crushed
2 cups frozen peas (or fresh)
800 g peeled and diced potatoes, par-cooked*
3 medium-sized, ripe tomatoes
2 tsp salt
1 tbsp tamarind paste**
2 cups water

First, place the tamarind paste in the water to soak. Break it up a little with your fingers as you do this. (Remove any seeds if you find them.)
Heat the oil in a heavy-based frypan. Saute the poppy and mustard seeds until the mustard seeds pop. Turn the heat down a little and saute the onions and garlic until they start to colour and soften.
Now add the other spices and the chillies, and saute gently for 5 minutes more.
Add the peas, potatoes, tomatoes, salt and the tamarind soaked in the water.
Stir well and simmer, covered, for 20-30 minutes (or microwave for an appropriate time). The potatoes should be quite tender but still hold their shape. You may have to add up to ½ cup more water during the cooking time.

Nutty Carrot Loaf

¾ cup roasted and salted peanuts
2 cups fresh wholemeal breadcrumbs
2 cups grated carrot (about 3 medium carrots)
1 tbsp fresh basil or oregano, chopped finely or 1 tsp dried
1 egg
3 tbsp (45 g) melted margarine or butter
3 tbsp fresh orange juice
¼-⅓ cup water (approx.)
1 tsp instant green herb stock
slice of lemon and a little parsley for garnish

Chop the peanuts in a food processor until they are quite finely chopped. Then place them in a bowl and mix with the breadcrumbs, carrot and basil.
Pre-heat the oven to 180°C.
Beat the egg and the melted margarine together with a fork and add to the bowl with the orange juice, water and stock. The mixture should have a 'sticky' consistency, but be neither too dry nor too wet.
Grease a loaf tin and line the bottom with butter paper cut to fit. Bake at 180°C for approximately 30 minutes or until the loaf is firm to the touch and has drawn away from the sides of the tin. Turn out and remove butter paper to serve, garnished with a lemon twist and a sprinkle of chopped parsley.

This loaf is not traditionally served with curries at all; in fact it's not really an Eastern dish. It does, however, complement curries beautifully. A delightfully nutty tasting and textured dish, it has more flavour than a dhal but is not at all overpowering.

This recipe is not recommended for microwaving or freezing.

Celery and Apple Sambal

1 cup finely chopped celery
1 medium-sized apple, unskinned and finely chopped
juice of 1 lemon

Place the celery and apple in a serving bowl and mix well with the lemon juice.

Plum or Prune Raita

1 cup plain yoghurt
½ cup fresh red plums, halved and stoned or ¼-½ cup chopped stoned prunes
½ tsp cinnamon

Mix the yoghurt and plums or prunes together, then sprinkle the cinnamon on top.

DESSERT

Apricot Crepes
Page 141.

Maharajah's Spiced Phyllo Parcels with Gruyere Sauce

Brown Rice with Parsley Garnish

Grape and Banana Raita

Tomato and Onion Sambal

Cheater's Mocha Mousse

This is a favourite dish which has met with unqualified approval. Crisp delicate phyllo pastry rolls with a curried vegetable and coconut sauce filling are topped with a subtle gruyere sauce. They look and taste wonderful, and they're not at all difficult to prepare.

*Silverbeet leaves may be used instead of spinach.

**Cover the phyllo you're not working with, with a dry tea towel. Damp tea towels often cause more sticky problems than they're worth; as long as you work steadily, the pastry won't dry out too much.

The sheets of phyllo may be cut in thirds, and 1 heaped tbsp of filling used instead of 2; these smaller parcels are ideal for an entree.

This recipe is unsuitable for microwaving. The parcels may be wrapped and frozen after baking and cooling. They may be frozen uncooked if well wrapped and brushed with melted butter. Cook in a hot oven without thawing.

Maharaja's Spiced Phyllo Parcels with Gruyere Sauce

200 g prepared spinach (stalks removed) chopped*
2 tbsp butter or ghee
1 medium onion, skinned and chopped
2 cloves garlic, crushed
1½ tsp fresh ginger, minced
1 capsicum, seeded and diced
1 tbsp commercial curry powder
½ tsp tumeric
2 medium potatoes, peeled and diced smallish
1 large carrot, grated
400 g cabbage, shredded (about ½ large cabbage)
1½ tsp salt
freshly ground pepper
1¼ cups coconut cream
18 sheets phyllo pastry — there are 27 sheets in a 375 g pack
70 g melted butter (approx.)

Microwave or steam spinach in a little butter (about 1 tsp) until just tender. Drain.

Melt the butter or ghee in a large heavy-based pan or pot and saute the onion, ginger, garlic, and capsicum until soft. Add the curry powder and tumeric and cook for 5 minutes, stirring, over a gentle heat.

Add the potatoes, cook for 8 minutes, then the rest of the vegetables. Lastly stir in the drained and chopped spinach. Now add the coconut cream and keep cooking over a gentle heat until most of the liquid has evaporated and the vegetables are tender. The mix should be quite dryish so that it doesn't seep through the pastry. Stir regularly while cooking.

Check seasoning.

Working on a floured surface, take 3 sheets of the phyllo pastry, spread on top of one other. Lightly brush the top sheet with melted butter.** (There's no need to butter each sheet.)

Cut the sheets in half, across their length.

Now place 2 heaped tablespoons of the filling onto each half. Starting at the end closest to you, fold in the edges of each strip and then roll up until you have a cylinder shape. Repeat this process until all the filling is used up — you should have 12 rolls.

Brush the tops well with melted butter (or ghee) and place seam side down onto a well-greased baking tray, leaving a small gap between each one.

Bake for about 30 minutes at 190°C until lightly golden.

Serve on a heated dish, topped by gruyere sauce.

Gruyere Sauce

60 g butter or margarine
⅓ cup plain flour
2 cups milk

¾ cup grated gruyere cheese*
1 small tsp salt
freshly ground pepper

Gruyere may be replaced by cheddar, but for this menu gruyere is worth making some effort to get.

Melt butter, stir in the flour then add the milk gradually, stirring all the time. Add a little more milk if needed; the sauce shouldn't be thick.
Bring to the boil, then stir in the seasoning and the gruyere.
Place on the table for everyone to serve themselves, or pour over the phyllo parcels immediately before serving.

This sauce may be microwaved.

Brown Rice with Parsley Garnish

3 cups brown rice
½ cup chopped parsley
water to come approximately 2.5 cm above the rice

Steam or microwave the rice, covered, until cooked. To steam, place the rice in a saucepan, cover with the cold water (2.5 cm (1 inch) above) and cover with a tight-fitting lid. Bring to the boil over a high heat, then immediately turn the heat right down, so that it is on but no more. Steam for approximately 35-40 minutes without removing the lid.*
Garnish the rice with the chopped parsley immediately before serving, or lightly fork it through.

Microwaving follows the same procedure, using plastic wrap or similar to cover, and cooking for a much shorter time (about 20-25 minutes).

Grape and Banana Raita

300 g black grapes   3 large bananas   ½ cup plain yoghurt

Place the grapes in a serving bowl and refrigerate until needed.
Just before serving, slice the bananas and mix with the yoghurt.
Toss with the grapes and serve immediately.

Tomato and Onion Sambal

500 g tomatoes, chopped
2 medium onions, skinned and chopped finely
1 tbsp lemon juice
1 tbsp olive oil
sprig of mint for garnish
salt to taste and a good grinding of black pepper

Have the onions prepared in advance. As close to serving time as possible, chop the tomatoes, mix gently with the onion, lemon juice and oil.
Season to taste and garnish with the mint.

DESSERT

Cheater's Mocha Mousse
Page 140.

Combination Curry

**Curried Mushrooms
and Spinach**

**Martinique Ginger and
Almond Tart**

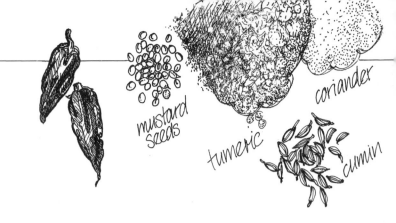

Curries are insidiously addictive, as many confirmed curry eaters can affirm. This is one of our favourites.

Yellow split peas are often used to make dhal, a 'cooling' mixture served with curries. In this case, however, they combine perfectly with potatoes to make a deliciously nutritious curry.

This curry is a very useful dish, quick and simple to make and very popular served with puris and/or rice, sambals, salads and other curry trappings.

*The curry may 'mush' a little cooked in this way, but this is perfectly acceptable.

**You will probably need to add the total amount of water, as the mixture tends to absorb it as it cooks.

You will find suggestions for sambals, raita and other curry side dishes on pages 162-163 and pages 113, 115.

Puris are wonderful served with this menu — turn to p. 161 for these.
Add a crisp green salad if you like, for colour and texture.

This recipe can be frozen for up to 1 month.

Combination Curry

1½ cups of urad dhal or yellow split peas
60 g butter or ghee
1 dsp mustard seed
1 large onion, peeled and finely chopped
3-4 small dried chillies, finely chopped
2 tbsp commercial curry powder
2 tsp coriander powder
1 tsp cumin
2 tsp tumeric
2 tsp salt
850 g potatoes, peeled and cubed
2-2½ cups water
½ cup liquid reserved from cooking the split peas

Either soak peas in water for at least 3 hours or overnight. Simmer, covered, for about 30 minutes or until soft.
OR cook in a pressure cooker for 10 minutes. This method requires no pre-soaking.*
Drained the cooked peas, reserving ½ cup of the cooking liquid.
Heat the butter, add the mustard seed and saute until it pops. An electric frypan is an ideal utensil. Add the onion and chillies and saute for a few minutes. Now add the curry powder, the other spices and the salt. Add the cooked drained dhal or split peas, then water,** reserved liquid from the split peas and the potatoes.
Stir well. Cover and simmer for 30-45 minutes (or microwave), stirring regularly so that it doesn't stick. The potatoes should be soft though recognisable, the peas forming a thick 'sauce' around them.

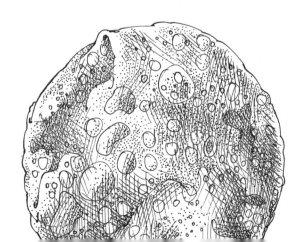

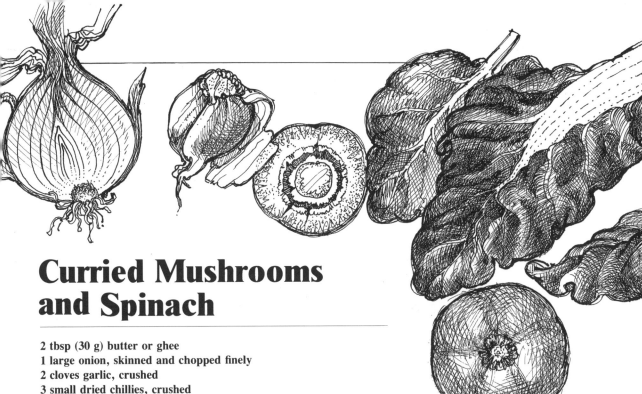

Curried Mushrooms and Spinach

2 tbsp (30 g) butter or ghee
1 large onion, skinned and chopped finely
2 cloves garlic, crushed
3 small dried chillies, crushed
1½ tbsp coriander
1 tsp cumin
½ tsp ground black pepper
500 g mushrooms, chopped
2 ripe tomatoes, chopped
1 tsp salt
¼ cup water
200 g spinach or silverbeet, stalks removed
½ cup plain yoghurt

Heat the butter or ghee in a large heavy-based pan over a gentle heat.
Saute the onion, garlic and chillies for 3 minutes, then add the coriander, cumin and pepper. Cook, stirring, for another 3 minutes.
Add the mushrooms and saute until they begin to produce liquid, then add the tomatoes and the salt.
Raise the heat to medium high and add the water. Stir and cook briefly.
Now add the chopped spinach or silverbeet leaves and mix well.
Cook, stirring, for a few minutes more, then turn the heat down again and add the yoghurt.
Combine well and heat through, then pour into a heated serving dish and serve.

This recipe is suitable for microwaving and freezes well, before the addition of the yoghurt, for up to 1 month.

DESSERT

Martinique Ginger and Almond Tart
Page 156.

Lima Bean Bobotie

Green Beans with Coconut

Raw Beetroot Salad with Orange Dressing

Fresh Fruit Platter

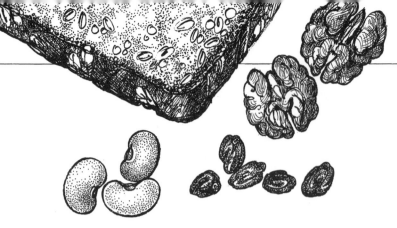

Bobotie is an African dish, but probably originated in Malaya and was taken to Africa by migrant workers several centuries ago. The original recipe uses lamb, but this wonderful dish uses lima beans instead.

*Don't replace the walnuts with other nuts if you can avoid it — they're delicious in this dish. But do check them for freshness before cooking with them; rancid nuts will ruin any dish.

Lima Bean Bobotie

150 g cubed wholemeal bread (3-4 slices)
300 ml (1¼ cups) milk
2 medium onions, skinned and chopped finely
2 cloves garlic, crushed
1 small capsicum, chopped (or 1 rib celery)
2 tbsp oil
2 tsp good curry powder (or more to taste)
1 tsp tumeric
1 tsp coriander
500 g cooked lima beans (3 cups cooked, about 1¾ cups raw)
½ cup currants or raisins
75 g (¾ cup) walnuts, roughly chopped*
1 tbsp chutney (mango or any fruit will do)
2 tsp salt
¾ cup (150 ml) vegetable stock or ¾ cup water with 1 tsp green herb stock added
3 eggs
1 cup milk
125g sour cream
1 tomato, chopped
1 tbsp parsley, chopped finely
freshly ground black pepper

Soak the wholemeal bread cubes in the warmed milk.
Saute the onions, garlic and capsicum in the oil until soft. Add to the frypan the curry powder, tumeric and coriander and stir over a gentle heat for 5 minutes. Add a little more oil if you need to.
Chop the lima beans roughly (with a knife — don't mash or blend) and add these to the frypan, along with the raisins and the walnuts. Cook a further 5 minutes.
Pre-heat the oven to 180°C.
Stir in the chutney, then the soaked bread cubes and milk. Add the salt, then place the mixture in a well-buttered 30 x 20 cm (12 x 8 inch) or similar baking dish. Spread out lightly, then pour over the vegetable stock.
Beat together the eggs, the sour cream, and the cup of milk. Add to this custard, the chopped tomato and parsley and the pepper.
Check the seasoning, then pour over the lima bean mixture.
Bake at 180°C for 40-45 minutes or until the top custard is firm and set (or microwave on medium for 15 minutes or until the top custard is set.)

Bobotie can be frozen for up to 1 month.

Green Beans with Coconut

1 small onion, sliced thinly
1 small capsicum, finely chopped
2 cloves garlic, crushed
1 cup dessicated coconut
1 tsp cumin
1 tsp coriander
½ tsp tumeric
1 tsp salt
4 tbsp (60 g) butter or ghee
500 g green beans, cleaned and sliced

Blend the first 8 ingredients, i.e., all except the butter and the beans, together in a processor, using the pulse button. Melt the butter or ghee over a gentle heat, then stir in the coconut/spice mixture. Cook for a few minutes, stirring, then add the green beans, cover and cook over a very gentle heat until the beans are tender, about 10 minutes (or microwave about 7 minutes).

Raw Beetroot Salad with Orange Dressing

½ cup freshly squeezed orange juice
¼ tsp grated orange rind
⅓ cup plain yoghurt
1 small clove garlic, crushed
250 g uncooked beetroot, peeled and coarsely grated
seasoning if desired, though this shouldn't be necessary

Beat together the orange juice, rind, yoghurt and garlic, then gently stir in the grated beetroot.
Chill for 30 minutes.
Serve on a bed of lettuce or spinach leaves

DESSERT

Fresh Fruit Platter
Over to you.

Summer Buffets

The following 6 recipes are intended as inspiration for buffet dishes, to be presented either individually or together. Each dish can be prepared ahead of time, with a minimum of fuss, and they all look and taste great. To complete a summer buffet table we suggest a large crisp green salad, and a choice from the salads on pages 49, 55, 69, 71 and 85.

This simple mousse looks quite stunning served with Fresh Tomato Dressing. It also makes a very attractive entree served with crispy French bread.
Fresh fruits such as grapes, strawberries, peaches, etc. make attractive and complementary side dishes.

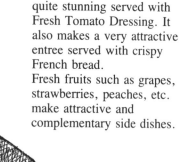
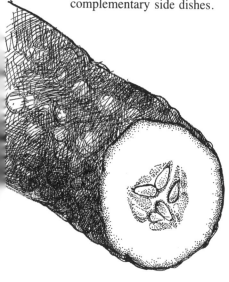

Classy Cucumber Mousse with Fresh Tomato Dressing

1 medium cucumber
½ medium onion, skinned
1 tsp salt
1 cup vegetable stock or 1 cup water plus 1 tsp green herb instant stock
1½ tbsp gelatine
4 tsp lemon juice
2 tsp capers, packed firmly
250 g cream cheese
1 cup cream
1 tsp (measured) freshly ground black pepper

Slice the unpeeled cucumber lengthwise, then scoop out the seeds with a teaspoon. Grate the cucumber and the onion, then place in a colander or sieve to drain for 20-30 minutes, while you prepare the rest of the ingredients.
Place the stock and gelatine in a bowl and heat, stirring, over boiling water until the gelatine has dissolved. Add the lemon juice and set aside to cool.
Chop the capers roughly. Place the cream cheese in a processor and blend, using the pulse button, while you pour in the cream. Add the chopped capers last with the freshly ground pepper, and blend until just mixed.
Scrape the cheese and cream mixture into a bowl.
Gently squeeze out the excess liquid from the drained cucumber/onion with the back of a spoon (or use your hands for maximum efficiency).
Add the drained and squeezed cucumber to the cheese and cream mixture.
Gently mix in the cooled gelatine/stock liquid.
Serve with Fresh Tomato Dressing spooned over attractively, and garnished with a small sprig of fresh dill if available.

Fresh Tomato Dressing

3 medium, firm, ripe tomatoes, peeled if desired
½ medium onion, skinned
2 large cloves garlic, crushed

1 tbsp wine vinegar
½ tsp salt
1 tsp freshly ground black pepper
½ cup oil, preferably olive

Place the quartered tomatoes, onion and garlic in a blender or processor and puree.
Add the vinegar, salt, pepper and oil and process until combined.

Piquant Pasta, Tofu and Nut Salad with Silverbeet

Pasta salads can sometimes be rather heavy and tasteless, but this one is lifted by the piquancy of the dressing, and the textural addition of the nuts and silverbeet.

300 g short pasta twists or spirals
250 g silverbeet, i.e. 3 large leaves, with stalks — 150 g prepared leaves
2 hard-boiled eggs, chopped
100 g roasted, salted peanuts or pine nuts
½ capsicum, preferably red
16 olives, preferably black

Cook the pasta according to the directions on the packet, then drain and refresh under cold running water. Set aside to drain thoroughly.
Remove the white stalks from the silverbeet and discard. Chop the leaves finely. Place in the bottom of quite a large serving dish.
Hard boil the eggs and roast and salt the peanuts if you only have raw on hand. Chop the hard-boiled eggs into bite-sized pieces.
Remove the seeds from the capsicum and cut the flesh into short strips.
Now place the very well drained, cooked pasta on top of the silverbeet in the serving bowl. Then add the eggs, capsicum and eggs, keeping the peanuts and olives until immediately before serving.
This dish can be refrigerated, covered, at this stage, until ready to serve.

Dressing

1 cup plain yoghurt
100 g tofu, chopped into 6 pieces*
3-4 cloves of garlic, crushed
2½ tsp runny or warmed honey
3 tbsp wine or cider vinegar
1 tsp salt
lots of freshly ground pepper

Place all the dressing ingredients in a food processor and blend until smooth.
Pour over the prepared salad immediately before serving and toss lightly.
Garnish with the peanuts and olives.

*The tofu could be replaced by cottage cheese, although the texture is not quite as good.

Some cubes or strips of cheese may be added to this dish if you wish.

121

No-Bake Savoury Cheese Pie

This appealing pie is ideal for a buffet table; each guest can help themselves to a wedge. It can also be served with a selection of fresh fruits, instead of a dessert or cheese board.

1 cup water cracker crumbs, such as Sao or cream
4 tbsp margarine or butter, melted
½ cup very well drained crushed pineapple (about ½ a 450 g tin)
1 cup (250 g) cream cheese
¼ cup chopped chives
½ cup cottage cheese
½ cup (125 g) sour cream
1 tbsp lemon juice
1 tsp Worcester sauce
⅓ cup grated or crumbled blue vein cheese (optional)
150 g fresh black grapes, quartered, pips removed
½-1 green or red capsicum, seeded and diced
⅓ cup roughly chopped walnuts
2 tbsp poppy seeds

Lightly butter the bottom and sides of a 20 cm (8 inch) springform cake tin.
Place the cracker crumbs in a small bowl. Melt the margarine and mix with the crumbs. Press firmly over the bottom of the greased cake tin.
Refrigerate until chilled and firm.
Drain and measure the crushed pineapple. Remove any excess liquid from the fruit by placing it in a sieve and then pressing gently with the back of a spoon.
Beat the cream cheese in a bowl with a spatula or wooden spoon until it is smooth and creamy (or beat in processor).
Now stir in all the remaining ingredients except the poppy seeds.
Place the cheese mixture into the chilled cracker base. Smooth the top over with a spatula, then sprinkle the top evenly with the poppy seeds.
Refrigerate until ready to serve.

This very easy salad looks spectacular on the buffet table. It must be made the day before serving, so it's ideal for pre-planning.

Jellied Beetroot Salad with Sour Cream Dressing

1 small onion, peeled and cut into quarters
1 small capsicum, seeded and chopped
1 stalk of celery, chopped

1 820 g tin beetroot or the equivalent fresh, cooked, reserving liquid
vegetable stock, preferably home-made or white wine or a mixture of both
¼ tsp ground cloves
½ tsp cinnamon
¼ tsp ground ginger
1 tsp salt
3 tbsp fresh lemon juice
2 tbsp sugar
freshly ground black pepper
3½ tbsp gelatine or agar-agar
sprigs of parsley as a garnish
sour cream dressing (see below)

Using a food processor or blender, put in the onion, capsicum, celery and three quarters of the tin of drained beetroot.
Reserve the juice, measure and place in a saucepan. Set a quarter of the beetroot slices aside.
Blend the ingredients in the processor until they are smooth.
Add enough vegetable stock or wine to the reserved beetroot liquid to make up a total of 4 cups.
Heat the liquid gently with the cloves, cinnamon, ginger, salt, lemon juice, sugar and pepper.
Remove 1 cup of this hot liquid and stir in the gelatine or agar-agar until it is completely dissolved. Return to a very gentle heat if necessary to achieve this.
Add the remaining 3 cups liquid to the mixture in the food processor and pulse 3-4 times.
Pour into a bowl and stir in the liquid gelatine mixture.
Rinse a 1 litre (1¾ pint) ring mould with cold water.
Cut up the remaining beetroot slices into semi-circles and place into the wetted mould.
Pour in the liquid beetroot and gelatine mixture. Leave it to cool completely, then place in a refrigerator overnight.
When you are ready to serve, loosen the edges with a knife, dip quickly into hot water, then invert onto a serving dish.
Fill the centre with sour cream dressing, and decorate with sprigs of parsley.

Sour Cream Dressing

1 cup sour cream
1 tbsp finely chopped onion
1 tbsp lemon juice
½ tsp salt

Process in the food processor or blender until smooth.

123

Indian Rice Salad with Fruit and Nuts

2 cups cold cooked rice, brown or white
1 small apple, cored and chopped
1 small capsicum, seeded and chopped
1 cup celery, finely chopped
1 small onion, peeled and finely chopped
¼ cup currants or raisins
1 cup chopped fresh or tinned yellow fruit such as peaches, pineapple, apricots or pawpaw
1 cup toasted nuts — almonds, cashews or peanuts
½ cup toasted sunflower seeds

Curry Mayonnaise Dressing

½ cup mayonnaise* (To make 1 cup: place 1 egg, 2 tbsp white wine vinegar, ½ tsp salt in food processor. Blend and then, with motor running, very slowly dribble in 1 cup oil through the feed tube.)

Then add:
2 tsp honey, runny or warmed
2 tbsp white wine vinegar
2 tsp good quality curry powder
2 tbsp salad oil
3 tbsp lemon juice (1 lemon)
2 cloves garlic, crushed
1½ tsp salt
¼ tsp chilli sauce
1 tsp freshly ground pepper

Mix together all the dressing ingredients with a fork or whisk until smooth.
Combine the rice with the vegetables, fruit and nuts.*
Stir in the Curry Mayonnaise Dressing.
Serve on a bed of torn lettuce, with the sunflower seeds sprinkled over the top. Garnish with slices of fresh fruit and sprigs of parsley.

Don't alter this recipe unless you really have to. Sue was taught how to make it while she was working in the Caribbean, and has perfected it over the years; it's luscious just as it is.

If preparing ahead, don't add the nuts until just before serving, as they will soften if left too long.

*Don't use commercial mayonnaise; it has quite a different flavour.

Guacamole

2 ripe avocados, peeled and mashed
1 firm, medium tomato, chopped
1 medium onion, peeled and chopped
1 tsp sugar
½ tsp coriander
1 small red chilli, fresh or dried, chopped — more to taste
salt and freshly ground black pepper to taste
2 tbsp olive oil
1 tbsp lemon juice

Place all the ingredients except the avocado and lemon juice in a food processor or blender and chop until smooth.
Stir this mixture into the mashed avocado. Slowly add the lemon juice. Adjust the seasoning.
Serve at room temperature.

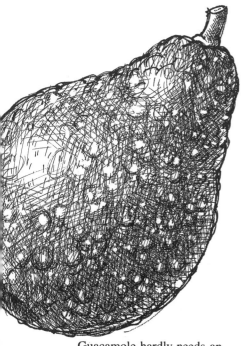

Guacamole hardly needs an introduction. Serve it with tortilla chips or whatever you fancy.

124

Mushroom and Garlic Dip

½ cup cottage cheese
150 g sour cream
75 g fresh, small mushrooms (don't use old ones as the flavour is too strong and they discolour the dip too much)
3 tbsp lemon juice
½ tsp freshly ground black pepper
salt to taste
4 good-sized cloves garlic, crushed
sprig of parsley for garnish

This dip is nice served with crudites or tortilla chips, etc. The garlic gives this dip its special tangy flavour, so don't reduce the number of cloves.

   Place all the ingredients in a food processor or blender and blend until creamy.
Cover and chill in a refrigerator for 2-3 hours.

Baba Ghanouj

Baba Ghanouj is a delicious Middle Eastern dip to serve with pita bread, crackers, etc. Don't omit the grilling/roasting procedures, as these give this dip its distinctive nutty, toasted flavour.

1 large or 2 medium eggplant(s) (500-600 g)
½ small onion, peeled and chopped in wedges
2 medium tomatoes, peeled and chopped
1 tsp brown sugar
1 tbsp olive oil
2 cloves garlic, crushed — more to taste
1½ tsp salt
2 tbsp lemon juice, more to taste
1 tsp freshly ground black pepper
2 tbsp tahini*
½ tsp chilli sauce — more to taste
1 tsp cumin

*Tahini can be purchased at specialty stores or refer to the recipe on p. 159.

   Pre-heat the oven to 190°C.
Either spear the whole, unpeeled eggplant(s) with a fork and hold over a gas flame or grill on all sides until the skin is flaky and blistered.
Peel off most of the flaked skin (but not all, it adds flavour) and slice the eggplant(s) into smallish wedges, about 5 cm (2 inches) in size.
Place the eggplant wedges into a shallow baking dish with the onion and tomatoes.
Sprinkle with the brown sugar, then drizzle over the 1 tbsp olive oil.
Bake at 190°C, uncovered, until the eggplant is soft and the tomatoes are slightly caramelised — about 40 minutes — but check regularly to prevent burning.
Place all the ingredients in a food processor with the garlic, salt, lemon juice, pepper, tahini, chilli sauce and cumin.
Process until all the ingredients are combined well.
Turn into a serving dish, cover with plastic wrap and chill well.

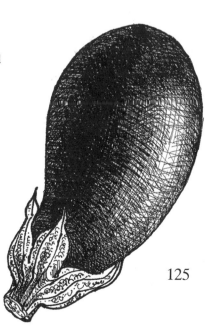

Desserts

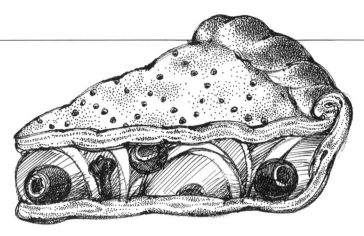

Granny's Double Crust Apple Pie

This is a very versatile recipe, as almost any fresh or canned fruit can be used for the filling. Fresh apple, of course, with its connotations of homeliness is best, but try adding ½ cup raw blueberries to it just for a change.

Shortcake Pastry

125 g butter
½ cup sugar
1 egg
4 tbsp cornflour
2¼ cups plain flour or 1¼ plain, plus 1 cup wholemeal flour
1 tsp baking powder

Cream the butter and the sugar, then beat in the egg. Sift in the dry ingredients and mix (if you are using a food processor you don't have to sift.)

The dough will be dryish, so don't add water unless you are certain it's needed, and then only a few drops at a time.

Refrigerate for 30 minutes if time permits.

Roll out half the dough to fit a greased, 23 cm (9 inch) pie or flan tin, preferably with a springform base. Set aside the other half of the dough for the top crust.

Filling

Cooked or tinned apples can be used in this recipe, but fresh are preferable for flavour and texture. Windfalls are not so successful as they tend to be dryish.

4 medium-sized apples such as Granny Smiths*
1½ tbsp lemon juice (about ½ a lemon)
½ cup fresh blueberries (optional)
3 tbsp brown sugar
6 whole cloves
1 tsp cinnamon

Pre-heat the oven to 180°C.

Peel and core the apples, slice them thinly and sprinkle with the lemon juice. Mix gently with the blueberries (if used).

Mix the brown sugar with the spices, then layer the fruit with the sugar/spice mixture into the prepared pastry base.

Roll out the other half of the pastry dough, and use it to top the pie.

Pinch the edges between finger and thumb to give a fluted effect, then prick the top lightly with a fork to prevent excessive rising.

Bake at 180°C for approx. 40 minutes, until the top is golden brown.

Dark Cherry and Walnut (or Almond) Strudel

A strudel with a difference — cherries and nuts enveloped in delicate phyllo pastry.

8 sheets of phyllo pastry
2 tbsp unsalted butter or more if needed*
1 425 g tin dark stoneless cherries drained and chopped - reserve the juice and set aside
4 tbsp brown sugar
2 tbsp raisins
1 tsp cinnamon
⅓ cup sour cream
2 tbsp cream cheese
2 tbsp kirsch or cherry liqueur or rum or orange juice
1 tbsp lemon juice
1 cup finely chopped walnuts or almonds
1 tsp orange rind
½ cup fresh breadcrumbs

*Unsalted butter really is preferable in this recipe if you can get it.

Stir the cherries, brown sugar, raisins and cinnamon together. Using a whisk or fork, beat together the sour cream, cream cheese and kirsch.
Add the chopped cherry mixture, the lemon juice, chopped nuts and orange rind.
Pre-heat the oven to 180°C.
Melt the butter and layer the phyllo sheets on a baking tray, brushing with unsalted butter between each layer.
Sprinkle the final layer with the fresh breadcrumbs (don't butter the final layer).
Spread the cherry and walnut mixture on top of the breadcrumbs, leaving a 4 cm (1½ inch) gap at each long end.
Fold these ends in, then roll up gently like a swiss roll.
Ensure that the roll sits seam side down on a baking sheet, and brush the top well with melted butter.
Bake at 180°C for 40-50 minutes until golden brown and crisp.
Serve hot, freshly sprinkled with icing sugar and accompanied by whipped cream.
Or serve with ice cream and the Cherry Sauce (see below).,

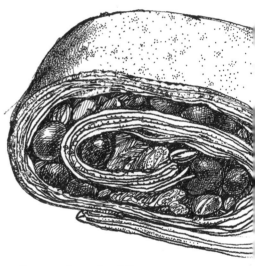

Because the ends of the strudel are folded in, they don't contain as much filling and are thicker than the rest of the dessert. You may like to reserve these ends for yourself if you have guests to serve.

Cherry Sauce

reserved juice from the tin of cherries
1 cup fresh orange juice
1 tsp cinnamon
¼ cup brown sugar
1½ tbsp cornflour mixed smooth with a little water

Place all the ingredients except the cornflour in a saucepan. Bring to the boil and simmer until the mixture is slightly reduced, about 10-15 minutes.
Stir in the dissolved cornflour and cook until thickened.

This page is dedicated to our friend and helpmate Mary, who invented and contributed the two chocolate pies which follow.
Always enthusiastically received, they're among our most popular desserts.

Mary's Chocolate and Orange Cream Pie

Base

75 g dark chocolate
3 tbsp butter
1¾ cup coconut

Melt the butter and chocolate over a low heat or microwave for 2 minutes.
Combine with the coconut.
Use the back of a spoon to press the base mixture into the bottom and part way up the sides of a 20 cm (8 inch) cake tin with removable sides. Chill until set.
If the tin does not have removable sides, line it with plastic wrap, leaving enough excess to overlap the sides.

Filling

1 dsp gelatine
½ cup fresh orange juice
50 g dark chocolate
2 tbsp sugar
1 315 g tin mandarins, drained
¾ cup lightly whipped cream
2 tbsp Sabra liqueur (optional)
2 tbsp toasted coconut for decoration
extra whipped cream

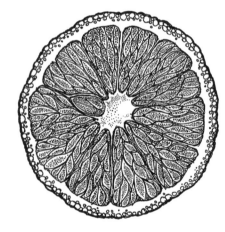

Soften the gelatine in 2 tbsp of the orange juice.
Melt the chocolate, sugar and the remaining orange juice over a gentle heat.
Remove from the heat and add half the drained mandarins, the gelatine mixture and the Sabra (if used).
Chill in the refrigerator until a soft jelly forms.
Lightly whip the cream then mix in the jelly until it is well combined.
Pour the filling mixture into the pie shell and place in the refrigerator to set.
To serve, remove the sides and base from the tin or lift the dessert out of the tin by holding the sides of the wrap. Gently peel off the plastic wrap and place the complete pie on a serving dish.
Decorate with the leftover mandarin segments and toasted coconut.
Serve with extra whipped cream.

Mary's Chocolate Coffee and Cream Pie

Base

75 g dark chocolate
3 tbsp butter
1¾ cup coconut

Melt the butter and the chocolate over a low heat or microwave for 2 minutes.
Mix with the coconut until well combined.
Use the back of a spoon to press firmly into the base and part way up the sides of a 20 cm (8 inch) cake tin with removable sides. If your tin does not have removable sides, line it with plastic wrap, allowing sufficient to overlap the sides.
Chill in the refrigerator.

Filling

1 cup water
1 tbsp gelatine
75 g dark chocolate
2 tbsp instant coffee
¼ cup brown sugar
2 tbsp Kahlua (optional)
1 cup cream

Soften the gelatine in 2 tbsp of the water.
Place the remaining water in a saucepan and heat with the chocolate, coffee, sugar, Kahlua (if used) and the gelatine. Stir until smooth and dissolved.
Pour into a bowl and chill in the refrigerator until a soft jelly forms.
Lightly whip the cream, then beat in the jelly.
Pour into the chilled pie shell and chill until firm.
Remove the sides and base of the cake tin or hold the sides of the plastic wrap and lift the pie from the tin.
Place on a serving plate.
Spread over the topping and serve.

Topping

1 cup cream
1 tbsp instant coffee
1 tbsp Kahlua (optional)

Whip the cream until soft peaks form, then beat in the coffee and lastly the Kahlua (if used).

Sour cream and plums, touched with spice and encased in a rich pastry, make this dessert a delightful blend of flavour and texture, but not too sweet.

Swiss Plum Tart

Pastry

1 cup plain flour
1 cup wholemeal flour
pinch of salt
150 g butter, cut into cubes
2 tbsp caster sugar
1 egg yolk
½ tsp vanilla essence

Place sifted flours and salt into a food processor (metal disc). Add the cubed butter and process for 30 seconds. Now add the sugar, the egg yolk and the vanilla and process very briefly, stopping as the dough begins to consolidate, just before it forms a ball.
By hand: Cut or rub the butter into the flours and salt until they resemble breadcrumbs. Then stir in the egg yolk, sugar and vanilla until a soft ball forms. Don't overwork the pastry.
Roll out the pastry to fit a lightly greased 23 cm (9 inch) pie or flan tin, preferably with a removable base. Chill for 30 minutes, then lay in a sheet of greaseproof paper, ensuring that the sides are covered, and cover the base with dried beans or rice.
Bake at 190°C for 10 minutes (i.e. bake 'blind').

Filling

1 850 g tin of Black Doris plums or the equivalent weight of fresh stewed plums
½ cup caster sugar
3 eggs
1 250 g carton sour cream
2 tbsp plain flour
2 tbsp kirsch (optional)

Topping

1 tsp cinnamon
1 tbsp icing sugar

Pre-heat the oven to 200°C.
Reserve the plum juice.
Halve the plums, removing the stones as you do so. Drain well in a colander.
Lay the plums, cut side down, into the cooled pie shell.
Whisk together the sugar and eggs until thick and creamy. Then add the sour cream, flour and kirsch and whisk together well.
Pour the cream mixture over the plums and bake at 200°C for 10 minutes, then reduce the oven temperature to 180°C and bake until the custard is set — this should take about another 25 minutes.
Remove from the oven, then leave for a few minutes before turning out.
Serve warm, sprinkled with the sifted cinnamon and icing sugar and whipped cream or with ice cream, and a sauce made from the reserved plum juice poured over.

Sauce

Mix the reserved plum juice with 1 tbsp cornflour which has been mixed with a little water until smooth.
Add 1 tsp sugar, ½ tsp cinnamon and 1 tbsp orange liqueur or orange juice.
Heat gently, stirring until thickened.

Eileen's Colonial Tart

Pastry

½ cup each of wholemeal and plain flour
½ tsp salt
75 g chilled butter, diced
¼ cup cold water (approx.)

Rub the butter into the flours and salt, or process briefly. Mix in the water until it starts to 'ball'. Place in plastic wrap and refrigerate 30 minutes if time allows, before rolling out.
Pre-heat the oven to 200°C.

Filling

1½ tbsp apricot jam (or sweet marmalade)
125 g butter
250 g (1 cup) sugar
2 eggs
2 lemons, grated rind and juice
2 medium-sized apples, preferably Granny Smith or cooking apples, grated

Line bottom and sides of the pie plate with the pastry and spread thinly with the jam.
Cream together the butter and the sugar, then drop in the eggs, one at a time.
Add the grated rind and juice of 2 lemons, then mix in the grated unpeeled apple.
Mix gently and spread evenly into the pastry lined dish.
Bake 35-45 minutes. (Cooking time will vary a little depending on the size and juiciness of the apples.) Check after 20 minutes and turn heat to 180°C if the crust appears to be browning too fast.
Serve at room temperature or warmed slightly, accompanied by whipped cream.

The appearance and flavour of this dish are much more sophisticated than the ingredients suggest. It came to us as the family favourite of a friend, whose father always jokingly said that it was the only t... he liked better than her mother!
It can be served either as part of a family meal, or as a delectable finish to a dinner with guests.

A very simple but attractive dessert with a lovely flavour combination.

Pear and Raspberry Upside Down Cake with Chocolate Sauce

Topping

25 g butter
½ cup brown sugar
½ tsp ground nutmeg
1 tsp ground ginger
½ cup chopped walnuts
1 425 g tin pears, drained (reserve 1 tbsp juice) or the equivalent weight of fresh pears, weighed when quartered, peeled and cored
1 425 g tin raspberries, or fresh stewed, drained

Melt the butter and stir in the brown sugar, the nutmeg and the ginger.
Spread over the base of a 20 cm (8 inch) round cake tin.*
Sprinkle in the walnuts. Place the pear halves or quarters on top of the walnuts, cut side up.
Pass the drained raspberries through a sieve, then pour evenly over the pears.
Try not to use a tin with a removable base, as you may lose dribbles of the topping into your oven!

It's best not to actually lay in the pears or raspberry puree until you have prepared the cake mix and can assemble the whole cake together.

Cake Mix

50 g butter
½ cup brown sugar
1 egg
¾ cup wholemeal flour
¾ cup plain flour
2 tsp baking powder
1 tbsp cocoa
⅔ cup milk
1 tbsp pear juice

Cream together the butter and the sugar until they are light and fluffy. Add the egg and beat again.
Place the wholemeal flour in a separate bowl, then sift the other dry ingredients into it. Mix well.
Fold into the creamed butter in 3 lots, alternating with the milk mixed with the pear juice.
Pour over the fruit and bake at 180°C for 30-40 minutes, or until firm. Invert the cake onto a serving plate.
Serve warm, with whipped cream, ice cream or a combination of either of these plus chocolate sauce. (The cake may also be served with custard.)

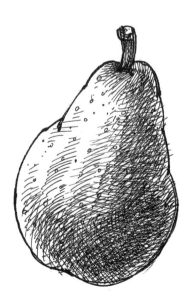

Chocolate Sauce

1 410 g tin evaporated milk
2 tbsp cornflour, mixed with 1 tbsp water
2 tbsp cocoa
1 tbsp butter
3 tbsp sugar
100 g dark chocolate
2 tbsp rum or ½ tsp vanilla

Place all the ingredients except the chocolate and rum or vanilla in a saucepan.
Beat well and cook, stirring over a gentle heat until well combined.
Melt in the chocolate, broken into small pieces, then stir in the rum or vanilla.
Don't bring to the boil.

A good chocolate sauce recipe is always valuable to have on hand — even if it's just used as a topping for ice cream served with fresh fruit and chopped nuts. It's very nice, however, teamed with the Pear and Raspberry Upside Down Cake.
This sauce makes a double quantity, using a whole can of evaporated milk, but any left over can happily be frozen for a later date.
You can, too, thicken some of the sweetened juice from the raspberries, to make a sauce, and then present the dessert with cream or ice cream topped with a swirl of both chocolate and raspberry sauce.

Old-fashioned Bread Pudding

This dessert takes about 5 minutes to prepare but tastes good enough to be served on any occasion — delicious!

5 medium slices wholemeal bread (about 150 g), buttered
½ cup chopped dates or prunes, pitted
2 tbsp currants
1 medium apple, unpeeled, grated
3 eggs
2 cups milk
½ tsp nutmeg
½ tsp cinnamon
3 tbsp brown sugar or honey

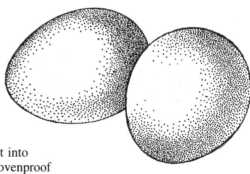

Pre-heat the oven to 180°C.
Leave the crusts on the bread. Butter lightly, then cut into cubes. Place in a buttered 30 x 20 cm (12 x 8 inch) ovenproof dish with the dates, currants and the grated apple. Mix lightly.
Beat together the eggs, milk and the spices. Add the brown sugar and beat again. Now pour this mixture over the cubed bread and fruits.
Bake at 180°C for 40-45 minutes.
Serve with vanilla ice cream or whipped cream.

Carrot Cake

This is a light, rather than moist, carrot cake. It's good not only as a dessert but also, of course, just for cutting and eating with a cup of coffee. This recipe makes a good-sized cake and keeps well (not that it will get much of a chance). If you're serving it as a dessert, cut it in generous squares and serve it with whipped cream if desired.

4 eggs
2 cups sugar
1 cup oil
2 tsp lemon juice
2 cups plain flour
1 cup wholemeal flour
2½ tsp cinnamon
1 tsp baking soda
3 tsp baking powder
½ tsp allspice
½-⅔ cup drained crushed pineapple
3 cups grated (or processor chopped) carrots
½ cup finely chopped almonds or walnuts

Pre-heat the oven to 180°C.
Using an electric beater, preferably, beat the eggs, sugar and oil together very well until they are thick and creamy.
Add the lemon juice, flours, cinnamon, baking soda, baking powder and allspice. Combine well.
Fold in the crushed pineapple, the carrots and the nuts. Mix well.
Pour into a greased 20 x 30 cm (8 x 12 inch) baking dish or similar (remember it makes quite a large quantity).
Bake at 180°C for approximately 1 hour.
Allow to cool in the baking dish, then ice with Cream Cheese Icing.

Cream Cheese Icing

4 tbsp (60 g) cream cheese
2 tbsp margarine or butter
2 cups icing sugar
1 tsp vanilla

Place all the ingredients in a food processor in the order given, then blend until whipped.

Eastern Coffee and Spice Gateau

A simply elegant dessert, this is quick to make but looks and tastes as if it has taken a lot more time and trouble.

Serve slices for dessert accompanied with whipped cream.

250 g (2 cups) plain flour
2 tsp baking powder
250 g (1 packed cup) brown sugar
100 g butter
1 egg
½ tsp vanilla
½ tsp baking soda
250 ml milk
2 tsp nutmeg
50 g (½ cup) finely chopped walnuts

Pre-heat the oven to 180°C.
Sift the flour and baking powder together. Combine with the brown sugar.
Rub in the butter until crumbly, then press half of the mixture firmly into a greased 20 cm (8 inch) round cake tin with a removable base.
Beat together the egg and the vanilla. Add the baking soda to the milk.
Stir the nutmeg into the remaining flour mixture.
Add the egg/vanilla mixture to the milk and baking soda, then pour this into the flour mixture and stir until well combined.
Pour on top of the base in the cake tin, then sprinkle the walnuts on top.
Bake at 180°C for 1 hour.
Allow to cool in the tin for 5-10 minutes. Turn out and top with the coffee icing and decorate with some whole unblanched almonds if desired.

Coffee Icing

1 cup icing sugar
2 tbsp sour cream or softened butter
1½ tsp instant coffee
½ tsp vanilla essence

Beat all the ingredients together until they are well combined and creamy.
Spread over the top of the cake, and decorate with whole unblanched almonds.

137

Super Ice Cream

This ice cream is very simply made in a food processor. Smooth and delicious, it needs no stirring or beating during the freezing process. This recipe serves 8-10, but it can very easily be halved.

The processor is important for beating the egg whites. An electric beater aerates the mixture to a greater extent, so that more water crystals are formed in the freezing process and the ice cream is likely to freeze too hard. Even if you wouldn't normally use your brand of processor to beat egg whites, you should have no trouble since this recipe has been tested using several different brands.

You should always add the flavouring ingredients to the whipped cream before combining with the egg whites. You can experiment yourself with variations of your choice. We've found that the addition of liqueurs causes this ice cream to crystallize slightly, as does the addition of water. Because of this, the addition of fresh fruits is not wholeheartedly recommended. Dried fruits, such as raisins, are fine, though, as are chopped nuts, etc.

Basic Vanilla Ice Cream

6 egg whites (use the yolks for mayonnaise, hollandaise sauce, etc.)
⅛ tsp salt
1 cup caster sugar (make your own in the processor)
3 cups cream — fresh or UHT may be used for this recipe, must be well chilled
1 tsp vanilla

Place the egg whites and salt in a food processor with the plastic beating attachment. Beat until the egg whites are stiff. Slowly beat in the caster sugar to form a stiff meringue. Remove the meringue from the processor and turn into a separate bowl. Scrape out the processor bowl well, using a rubber spatula.
Place the cream into the food processor bowl, and beat until just stiff enough to hold a soft peak. Add the vanilla and combine. Fold the whipped cream gently into the meringue mixture until they are well mixed.
Pour the mixture into a freezer container (preferably plastic) and freeze, covered, until firm.

Variations

1. Coffee — Simply add 1 dsp instant coffee to the whipped cream instead of the vanilla. Chopped nuts and/or raisins are nice additions too.
2. Chocolate — add 2 tbsp sifted cocoa to the whipped cream instead of the vanilla.
3. Tutti Frutti — fold in ½ cup chopped nuts and 1 cup mixed glace cherries, candied peel, raisins and candied pineapple.
4. Coconut — 1 cup of toasted coconut added to the whipped cream with the vanilla.
5. Chocolate Chip and Marshmallow — fold 1 cup chocolate chips and ½ cup chopped marshmallows into the whipped cream before mixing with the meringue.
6. Cassata — this classic Italian dessert is well worth making. To make it successfully, however, you should make the basic ice cream recipe in 3 separate lots, using a third of the recipe each time, i.e. use the same procedure, but 2 egg whites, 1 cup cream, a tiny pinch salt, and ⅓ cup caster sugar.
Make up the first mixture, add ½ tsp vanilla to the whipped cream and combine well. Spread into the bottom of a round 20 cm (8 inch) cake tin with removable sides. Cover and freeze.
Make up the second mixture, add 2 tsp sifted cocoa to the whipped cream and combine well. Spread on top of the first mixture, cover and freeze.
Make up the third mixture, add 2 tbsp chopped nuts, plus ⅓ cup mixed glace cherries, candied peel, raisins and candied pineapple.
Spread this third mixture on top of the other 2.
Cover and freeze until ready to turn out and serve.

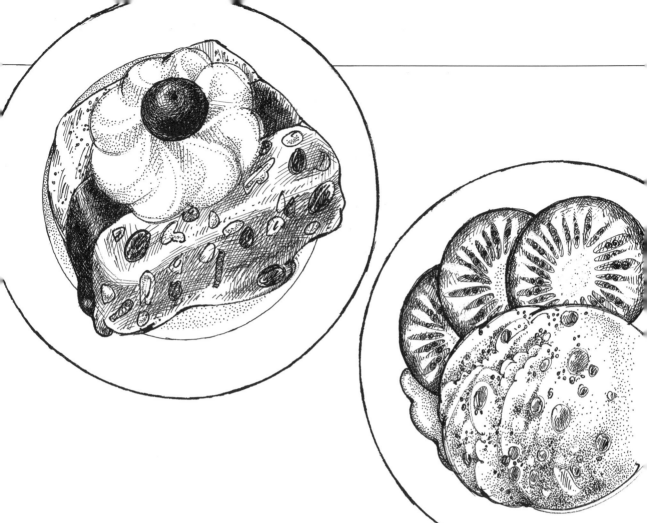

Fruit Sorbet

½ cup water
¾ cup caster sugar
juice of 1 medium lemon
2 cups of fruit pulp or puree or pure fruit juice
1 tbsp liqueur (optional)*
1 egg white

Heat the water, the sugar and the lemon juice in a saucepan over a medium heat until the sugar is dissolved. Allow to cool. Pass the fruit pulp or juice through a sieve. Combine with the cooled syrup and liqueur (if used). Place in a covered container in the freezer until frozen.
Remove from the freezer. Beat the stiffly beaten egg white into the fruit mixture with a whisk or similar, breaking down the ice crystals as much as possible.
Return to the freezer immediately, until ready to serve.

If the sorbet is still too full of ice particles when you are ready to serve, pile the sorbet quickly into the processor and pulse for a few seconds.
Dish up into sorbet glasses and serve.
Sorbet may be served over ice cream and/or accompanied by fresh fruit, etc.

Sorbets are a light dessert, ideal after a heavier meal. The flavour is full bodied and most appealing when it follows a rich or spicy meal. Quick and easy, too. Fruit suggestions are raspberry, apricot, orange, kiwifruit, etc.

If you are using tinned fruit and syrup for the sorbet, cut the sugar down to ½ cup.

*1 tbsp liqueur may be added, e.g. Grand Marnier with apricot or orange sorbet, or the liqueur can be poured over the sorbet immediately before serving.

139

This pie is an old favourite. The golden crust contains a caramel-like filling, finished with a subtle nutty topping.

Pecan Pie

Line a 23 cm flan tin with short crust pastry (p. 173).

Filling

1 cup packed brown sugar
½ cup white sugar
1 tbsp flour
2 eggs
2 tbsp milk
1 tsp vanilla
½ cup (70-80 g) melted butter
1 cup pecan nuts (raw unsalted cashews will do, or even walnuts)

Pre-heat the oven to 180°C.
Mix the sugars and flour together.
Add the eggs and beat well, then add the milk, vanilla and the melted butter.
Fold in the shelled nuts, roughly chopped, and pour into the pastry-lined flan or pie plate.
Bake at 180°C for 40-50 minutes, but check at 30 minutes to ensure that it's not cooking too fast.
Serve warm, in wedges, accompanied by whipped cream

This mousse looks and tastes great, but is so quick and simple to prepare — ideal when you're short of time. Chocolate mousse can be prepared from this recipe by replacing the coffee with 2 tbsp cocoa and adding an extra 2 tbsp caster sugar.

Cheater's Mocha (or Chocolate) Mousse

1 tbsp gelatine
1 tbsp instant coffee
½ cup boiling water
1 410 g tin evaporated milk, very well chilled
1 tsp vanilla
½ cup caster sugar
cream and chopped nuts for garnish

Place the gelatine and coffee in a small bowl and mix. Pour in the boiling water and stir until the gelatine is dissolved.
Place the bowl in a little cold water in the sink to cool. (Don't let it set, though — 5 minutes will do.)
Whip the chilled evaporated milk until it is thick and frothy, preferably with an electric or hand beater. The milk should double in size.
Add the sugar slowly, beating all the time, then the vanilla.
Pour in the cooled coffee/gelatine mixture and beat again, until thoroughly mixed.
Chill in individual parfait or large wine glasses, topped with whipped cream and a sprinkle of chopped nuts.
Or pour into a ring jelly mould to set. Chill, then turn out onto a serving plate. Top with whipped cream and chopped nuts and accompany with fresh fruit if desired.

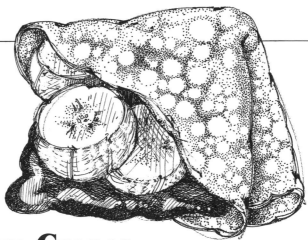

Banana/Rum Crepes

Crepes

(makes approx. 12 crepes)
1 cup plain flour
1 tbsp caster sugar
1½ cups milk
2 tbsp melted butter
2 eggs
1 tsp vanilla

Place the flour and sugar in the processor bowl (or blender).
Beat or whisk together the milk, melted butter, eggs and
vanilla.
With the motor running, pour the milk mixture slowly into the
feed tube.
Turn off the motor and pour the batter into a bowl. Let it rest
for 30 minutes.
Heat a greased 15 cm (6 inch) crepe pan* on medium high.
Pour about 2 tbsp batter into this and swirl the mixture quickly,
to make a thin coating of batter on the bottom of the pan.
Loosen the edges with a spatula and turn over once bubbles
start to appear and the bottom is a golden brown. Cook the
other side.
Repeat the process, greasing the pan with a little butter
between each crepe.
Remove from the pan and stack on top of each other.

Filling

30 g butter
8 medium bananas, cut into 5 cm (2 inch) chunks
juice of 1 medium lemon
**2 tbsp rum (or orange juice, though the rum does make this
particular recipe really special)**
1 tbsp brown sugar

Melt the butter in a large frypan.
Add the remaining ingredients and cook for 5 minutes over a
gentle heat.
Fill each crepe and fold over into 4.

Serve with whipped cream and ice cream and extra sliced
bananas for garnish.

These crepes make a truly
lovely dessert. While we've
chosen the banana/rum
combination here, this recipe
lends itself to use with
other fruit as well, such as
fresh apricots, apples or
strawberries. Tinned fruit
may be used if fresh are not
available.

**Keeping a crepe pan just for
this purpose is a good idea;
your crepes will then be
much more successful.
Crepes can be made in
advance. Fill them, then heat
in a hot oven or microwave
just before serving.*

141

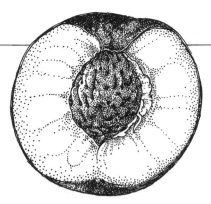

The fruit for this quick and easy crumble can be varied according to what you have in hand, or what fresh fruit are in season. The topping is truly delicious, however, so we recommend making this dessert in a 20 x 30 cm (8 x 12 inch) baking dish or similar, so that there's as much topping as possible on top of each individual portion (it's crunchier this way, too).

If you're using bananas instead of the blueberries, you will need to add 3 tbsp of peach juice to the fruit as well, to ensure it doesn't dry out.

Peach and Blueberry Crumble

1 820 g tin sliced peaches, drained or the equivalent amount of fresh fruit, stewed
1 cup of fresh blueberries or sliced bananas (about 3 medium)*
1 tbsp fresh lemon juice

Crumble Topping

75 g butter
½ cup wholemeal flour
½ cup desiccated coconut or rolled oats
1 tsp cinnamon
¾ cup brown sugar

Pre-heat the oven to 190°C.
Lightly butter a 20 x 30 cm (8 x 12 inch) baking dish.
Lay in the drained tinned or stewed peaches, mixed with the blueberries.
Sprinkle the lemon juice over the peaches and blueberries. If you're using bananas, sprinkle them with the lemon juice before adding.
Place all the crumble ingredients into the bowl of a food processor and process until mixed.
Sprinkle the crumble over the top of the fruit, and bake at 190°C for 45 minutes, or until the topping is crisped and golden.

Variations

Fresh, grated apples, unpeeled — we suggest 3 medium apples plus 1 cup of any berry fruit.
Plums — about 800 g fresh stewed or tinned, plus 1 cup of any berry fruit.
Blueberries — about 4 cups of fresh berries, used uncooked.

American Fudge Brownies

¾ cup margarine or butter (180 g)
1½ cups brown sugar
1½ tsp vanilla
3 eggs
½ cup plain flour
¼ cup wholemeal flour
½ cup cocoa
½ tsp baking powder
½ tsp salt
¼ cup chopped nuts or ¼ cup raisins or a combination of both

Pre-heat the oven to 180°C.
Melt the margarine or butter and using a wooden spoon, blend
it with the sugar and vanilla in a mixing bowl.
Add the eggs, and beat well with the spoon.
Combine the flour, cocoa, baking powder and salt and
nuts/raisins.
Gradually stir into the egg mixture until well blended. Spread
into a buttered 20 cm (8 inch) square cake tin.
Bake at 180°C for 30-40 minutes or until the brownie begins to
pull away from the sides of the pan.
Cool and cut into squares.
If desired, top with chocolate icing, before cutting up.

Chocolate Icing

25 g butter, softened
2 tbsp icing sugar
1 dsp cocoa
½ tsp vanilla essence

Beat all the above ingredients together until smooth and
spread over the cooled brownie in the pan or simply dust the
brownies with sieved icing sugar or leave them plain.

These brownies, made in a
few moments, are wonderful
to whip up for unexpected
guests, to take on a picnic or
bake whenever you fancy
something chocolaty and
sweet.

143

Lemon meringue pie is a most luxurious dessert which is neither difficult to prepare nor expensive. Don't expect there to be any left over, however — it's everybody's favourite.

You do need an electric beater to beat the meringue sufficiently. A small hand-held one is perfectly adequate.

Lemon Meringue Pie

Pastry

To line a 23 cm (9 inch) pie or flan plate, peferably with a removable base.

½ cup wholemeal flour
½ cup plain flour
75 g butter (chilled)
¼ cup ice or cold water (approx.)

Place the flours then the butter, cut into 6 pieces, into a food processor.
Process, using the pulse button, adding the water through the feed tube at the same time — 3-4 short bursts should be enough. The mixture will begin to 'ball'.
Form a ball from the dough, wrap it in plastic and chill in the refrigerator for 30 minutes if time permits.
Pre-heat the oven to 200°C.
Roll out the pastry to fit the greased pie plate, bottom and sides.
Fit a piece of tin foil into the base, taking care also to cover the sides of the flan.
Into this pour 2 cups raw rice.
Place the base in the pre-heated oven, then turn the heat down to 190°C.
Bake 'blind' for 20-25 minutes, then remove the rice and tin foil. Bake for another 5 minutes.
Remove from the oven and cool.

Filling

2¼ cups water
½ cup sugar
grated rind of 2 large or 3 medium lemons
1 tbsp butter
4 tbsp cornflour, generous
4 egg yolks
juice of 2 large or 3 medium lemons

Bring the water to the boil with the sugar, lemon rind and butter.
Boil for a few minutes, stirring.
Blend the cornflour with a little cold water and mix in, stirring all the time and cook for at least 3 minutes.
Remove from the heat and add the well-beaten egg yolks and the lemon juice.
Leave to cool before you prepare the meringue. Pre-heat the oven to 140°C.

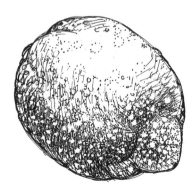

Meringue Topping

Beat the whites of 4 eggs until they stand up stiffly in peaks.
Gradually add 1 cup caster sugar, in 3 lots, beating
continuously.* Don't hurry this stage.
The meringue at this stage should be very thick, like mobile
marshmallow.
Now pour the filling into the base and pile the meringue on top.
Bake in a cool oven, 140°C for 30-40 minutes.
Serve at room temperature, accompanied by fresh whipped
cream.

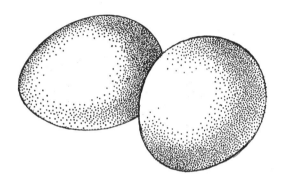

Individual Meringues

4 egg whites (use the yolks for mayonnaise, etc.)
1½ cups caster sugar
1 tsp vanilla essence
1 tsp white vinegar
2 tsp cornflour
1 dsp boiling water

Pre-heat the oven to 120°C.
Beat the egg whites with an electric beater until they stand up
in peaks. (An egg beater is not recommended as it's very hard
work.)
Add the caster sugar in 4 lots, beating all the time and beating
well between each addition.
The mixture should be thick and stiff, like a very thick
marshmallow.
Add the rest of the ingredients and beat in, adding the water
last.
Place in spoonful lots according to how large you want your
meringues to be (we pefer to use a heaped tablespoon) onto a
wet, greased oven tray.
Bake for 30 minutes at 120°C, by which time the outsides of
the meringues should feel crisp to the touch. (You won't need
quite so long if your meringues are smaller.)
Remove from the oven and place on a cake rack until cold.
Store in an airtight tin.

Meringues are always useful,
and have the advantage that
they can be made in advance
and kept in an airtight tin.
These meringues are very
simple to make and have a
crisp outer casing, with a
marshmallow middle.
Serve them on their own for
dessert, put them together
with whipped cream, or serve
them with a light dessert such
as a mousse or flummery.
Fresh strawberries, meringues
and cream are a wonderful
combination, or use any other
fresh or tinned fruit.

145

This moist, rich torte is a chocolate lover's delight, and a perfect finish to any meal.

Chocolate Almond Torte

200 g dark chocolate
200 g butter
1 tbsp cocoa
200 g (1 cup) caster sugar
125 g (1 cup) plain flour, sifted
50 g (½ cup) ground almonds
4 eggs, separated

Pre-heat the oven to 190°C.
Melt the chocolate and the butter together in a bowl over a pot of hot water (or for 4 minutes on medium low in a microwave). Stir in the cocoa until the mixture is smooth.
Beat the caster sugar and egg yolks with a whisk or beater until they are thick and creamy. Stir in the chocolate mixture.
Mix the flour and almonds together until they are well combined, then gently add them to the chocolate mixture.
With a clean whisk or electric beater, beat the egg whites until they are stiff but not dry. Fold them carefully into the chocolate mixture.
Pour the mixture into a greased and lightly floured 23 cm (9 inch) round cake tin, preferably springform (removable base)*. Bake at 190°C for 30-40 minutes. The centre should still be a little moist when tested with a skewer, but not runny. Remove the torte from the oven and let it cool completely in the tin on a cake rack.
Now turn the torte out and pierce the top of the cake all over with a skewer.
Using a teaspoon, pour the following mixture over the top of the cake.

If you don't have a springform tin, line the bottom of the tin with some butter or greaseproof paper. A 20 cm (8 inch) tin may be used, but increase the cooking time to 45-50 minutes.

2 tbsp rum
3 tbsp milk, stirred together.

Now place the cake in the refrigerator to chill while you're making the glaze.

Glaze

75 g dark semi-sweet chocolate
3 tbsp butter, unsalted
1 tbsp strong liquid coffee

Melt the glaze ingredients together in a microwave on medium low for 4 minutes, or in a bowl over hot water. Beat well, then pour over the cold cake, using a knife or spatula to spread around the sides.
Keep the torte refrigerated, where it will keep well for up to 2 weeks covered with foil or plastic wrap. Serve at room temperature, though.

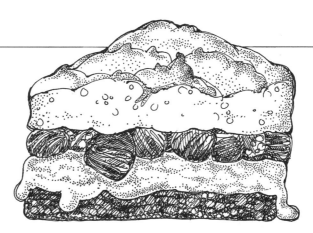

Baked Alaska with Fruit

1 round 20 cm (8 inch) sponge, cut in half horizontally to give 2 identical rounds
1 litre of ice cream, softened slightly, the flavour of your choice
1 cup crushed, well-drained pineapple or stewed drained apricots, fresh sliced strawberries, etc.
3 egg whites, stiffly beaten
½ tsp vanilla
½ cup caster sugar

Line the bottom of a 20 cm (8 inch) round cake tin (removable sides), with a round of greaseproof paper.
Fit one half of the sponge cake into the prepared tin. Wrap the other half in plastic and freeze for another use. Slice the ice cream to fit on top of the sponge and smooth well.
Cover with plastic wrap or similar, then place in the freezer and freeze until very firm.
Pre-heat the oven to very hot, 250°C.
Using an electric beater, beat the egg whites until stiff, then add the sugar in 2 lots.
Add the vanilla and continue beating until the meringue is very thick and stiff.
Turn out the ice cream cake from the cake tin. Remove the greaseproof paper from the bottom of the cake and place on an ovenproof serving dish.
Working quickly, spread the fruit evenly over the top of the ice cream.
Cover with the meringue entirely, top and sides.
Bake at 250°C for 5 minutes; the meringue will be a delicate brown at this stage.
Serve immediately.

Baked Alaska is such a simple dessert, but looks impressive and tastes superb. Its attraction lies in the freshly cooked meringue topping which is perfectly offset by the still firm ice cream beneath. It must, however, be baked exactly according to instructions and served immediately or the ice cream will melt.

Don't discount pavlova as a dessert, just because it's an old Kiwi favourite. It's just as popular as ever, and very simple to make.

The secret is in the beating of the egg whites; this must be done thoroughly and without haste, so that the resulting meringue is very thick and ponderous, like marshmallow before it sets. A small hand-held electric beater is perfectly adequate for this task, but a hand beater is not recommended.

Pavlova

5 egg whites
1¼ cups caster sugar
1 tsp vanilla essence
1 tsp white vinegar
300 ml cream for topping and decoration
fresh fruit, etc., of your choice (see topping)

Pre-heat the oven to 140°C.

Separate the eggs and place the whites in a large bowl. Make sure that no water or yolk has managed to make its way into the bowl, i.e. use dry utensils and remove any yolk if necessary.

Beat the egg whites until soft peaks form.

Add ⅓ cup sugar, then beat until this is dissolved.

Gradually add the remaining sugar, beating well after each addition.

Remember that this process should not be hurried and should take about 10 minutes to achieve.

At this point the mixture should be thick and marshmallow-like. Now add the vanilla and the vinegar, and beat for 1 minute to combine.

Line an oven tray with lightly greased paper, and dust lightly with cornflour.

Mark an 18 cm (7 inch) diameter circle on the tray, then spoon the meringue into the circle, smoothing it out to the edges. The sides should be approximately 8 cm (3 inches) in height.

Smooth the top and sides of the pavlova, using a flat knife blade. Then 'groove' the sides if you wish, and flatten the top again.

Turn the oven down to 130°C, then bake the pavlova for 1½ hours. It should be slightly crisp on the outside, not sticky. If, after an hour of cooking, it feels sticky to the touch, turn the oven up to 140-150°C for the last half-hour of cooking.

Allow the pavlova to cool on the tray.

The top will almost always fall, so it is advisable to take a sharp knife and cut around the edge of the top. The crisp meringue will drop slightly, onto the marshmallow filling, giving room for the topping of your choice.

Gently ease the pavlova off the greaseproof paper at this point, using a spatula and place on a serving dish.

Topping

Whip the cream, and spread over the top of the pavlova.
You can top this with:
— sliced bananas mixed with passionfruit pulp,
— sliced strawberries, tossed with a warmed strawberry or raspberry jam and a little rum or brandy
— or anything else you fancy.

Fresh Fruit Fritters

Slices or rings of fresh fruit coated in batter and deep fried are a very quick but always popular dessert. All fruit should be fresh, not tinned or cooked.

Fruit Suggestions

sliced bananas
apple rings, peeled or unpeeled
pineapple rings (these could be tinned, but would have to be very well drained)
halved apricots
whole strawberries
whole grapes
sliced kiwifruit

Batter

⅓ cup plain flour
⅓ cup cornflour
½ tsp baking powder
⅔ cup milk
2 tsp caster sugar
pinch of cinnamon
½ tsp vanilla
1 egg*

If you want an even lighter batter, separate the egg and beat the white stiffly. Fold in last.

Beat the batter ingredients altogether with a whisk or electric beater until well combined.
Leave to stand for 30 minutes.
Dip the prepared fruit into the batter, so each piece of fruit is coated.
Deep fry in hot oil (refer to specific instructions with Tempura recipe p. 108 if unsure) for 1-2 minutes or until the batter is golden brown.
Drain on kitchen paper and serve immediately, dusted with icing sugar if you wish. Accompany with whipped cream and/or ice cream.

This wonderful Italian trifle cake is very easy to make but looks stupendous. It's ideal for a dinner party as it can be entirely assembled the day before, and if you use bought sponges, it will take about half an hour to assemble.

Italian Trifle Cake

Buy or make 2 23 cm (8 inch) sponge cakes. They should be slightly stale and firm (it's a good idea to keep a couple in the freezer just for this.)
Cut each sponge into 2, using a long serrated knife, so that you have 4 'rounds'.

Filling

2 tbsp cornflour
2 tbsp custard powder
3 tbsp sugar
1 cup cream
1 cup milk
1 tbsp orange or almond liqueur (optional)
1 450 g tin crushed pineapple = 1 cup well-drained fruit or use an equivalent amount of fresh sliced strawberries, apricots or other
2-3 tbsp apricot jam or marmalade, warmed (or strawberry jam if using strawberries, etc.)
¼ cup rum or brandy mixed with ½ cup milk or
¾ cup reserved pineapple liquid or similar

Topping

1 cup cream
2 tbsp icing sugar
1 tsp vanilla
1 cup toasted coconut or toasted slivered almonds

Place the cornflour, custard powder, sugar, cream and milk in a saucepan and mix until smooth. Bring to the boil, stirring constantly.
Reduce the heat and cook, still stirring, for 5 minutes.
Gently stir the well-drained crushed pineapple (or fruit of your choice) into the custard mixture and allow at least 10 minutes to cool. (Place the pot in a sink of cold water if you're in a hurry.)
Place the first layer of sponge on a serving plate.
Using a teaspoon, spoon over a quarter of the rum mixture.
Spread over a thin layer of jam, then a third of the fruit custard mixture.
Set the next layer of sponge on top, spoon on a quarter of the rum, spread with jam and then the next third of the fruit custard.
Repeat once more, then top with the last layer of sponge cake and spoon over the remaining rum.
Chill the cake while whipping the cream until stiff with the icing sugar and the vanilla.
Spread the whipped cream over the top and sides of the cake; then sprinkle the entire cake with either toasted coconut or toasted slivered almonds.
Chill for at least 6 hours.
Serve with a garnish of fresh fruit if wished, e.g. strawberries if you use strawberries, etc.

150

Instant Sponge

2 cups self-raising flour*
pinch of salt
1 cup caster sugar
3 eggs
3 tbsp milk
75 g butter, melted and cooled a little

Grease the cake tin(s) and dust with flour. Line the bottom of each with greased greaseproof paper. Pre-heat the oven to 190°C.
Place all the ingredients in a food processor for about 40 seconds or alternatively place all the ingredients in a bowl and beat with an electric beater for 2 minutes.
Pour into cake tin(s) and hollow the centre slightly.
Bake for 20-30 minutes or until a skewer comes clean.
Turn out onto a wire rack, and cool.

This recipe for a quick and easy butter sponge cake is a very useful one to have on hand. While it doesn't produce a particularly feather light creation, it is ideal for use in trifles, fruit sponges, gateaux, etc.
The quantity of batter makes 2 round 20 cm (8 inch) cakes or one 30 x 23 cm (12 x 9 inch) square.

*The self-raising flour can be replaced with 2 cups of plain plus 2 tsp baking powder.

Quick and Easy Apple Cake

2 cooking apples (medium to large Granny Smiths are ideal)
1 cup brown sugar
125 g butter
1 egg
½ cup raisins or sultanas
1¼ cups wholemeal flour
1 tsp baking soda
1 tsp cinnamon
½ tsp allspice
½ tsp nutmeg

Pre-heat the oven to 180°C.
Peel, core and chop the apples thinly. Place in a bowl and cover with the sugar.
Melt the butter, then blend the egg in with a fork. Add to the apples and sugar.
Stir in the raisins and the sifted dry ingredients, until just mixed.
Line the bottom of a ring tin or 20 cm (8 inch) round tin with butter or greaseproof paper.
Pour in the cake mixture and spread evenly.
Bake at 180°C for 35-45 minutes, or until a skewer inserted into the middle of the cake comes out clean. (The timing can depend on how fresh/juicy your apples are.)
Note: If you are using plain flour, the cake will take between 50 and 60 minutes to cook.
Turn out onto a cake rack, remove the butter paper and cool.
Serve at room temperature or warm, dusted with icing sugar and accompanied by whipped cream.

This cake can be prepared so quickly and tastes so good, that it deserves some kind of recognition as a 'best' cake. It makes a quick and delicious dessert, and the recipe — the origins of which are unknown as it has been passed down the family — is almost always requested by those who sample it.

This strawberry shortcake is quite different in that it is filled with strawberries folded into a custard then baked. Fresh strawberries are also used to garnish the cake. This is a delicious recipe which always receives rave reviews.

Instead of strawberries, when they're not in season, you can use cooked or canned apples, peaches, apricots, etc. Use a jam made from the same fruit as you are using (see recipe) and decorate with fresh fruit if at all possible.

Strawberry Shortcake

100 g butter
¾ cup caster sugar
1 egg
½ tsp vanilla essence
1 cup plain flour
½ cup wholemeal flour
1 tsp baking powder

Cream the butter and sugar, add the egg and vanilla and beat well. Add the flours and baking powder and mix until smooth — this can all be done in a food processor, otherwise sift the plain flour and the baking powder.
Turn the dough out onto a lightly floured surface and knead lightly.
Divide the dough into 2 almost equal halves — allow just slightly more dough for the bottom half, as it has to extend up the sides of the tin about 2.5 cm (1 inch). Refrigerate the dough for at least 15 minutes, if possible.
Flour each half. Place the bottom part of the shortcake between 2 sheets of greaseproof paper and roll out to fit a 20 cm (8 inch) round cake or flan tin, preferably with a removable base. Ease the dough into the tin.
Roll out the second half of dough to fit, but allow it to remain on the greaseproof paper. Refrigerate both top and bottom until you are ready to assemble with the filling.

Filling

1 punnet fresh strawberries, hulled (450-500 g) — slice half for the filling, but keep the rest whole for decoration
3 tbsp sugar
1 tbsp water
1 cup cream
2 tbsp custard powder
1 tbsp cornflour
½ cup milk
2 tsp strawberry jam
1 tbsp kirsch liqueur (optional)
1 tbsp caster sugar

Place the sugar in a heavy-bottomed pot with the water. Cook over a gentle heat, stirring only once or twice to dissolve the sugar, until it begins to turn very faintly golden. (If you overstir, you risk the sugar crystallising — at which point you will have to start again!)
Remove from heat and stir in the cream.
Mix the custard powder and cornflour with the milk, until smooth, then add these slowly to the syrup and cream, stirring as you do this.
Return the saucepan to a gentle heat and bring to the boil, stirring constantly, until thick and smooth. Allow to cool, at least a little.
Pre-heat the oven to 190°C.

Stir in the strawberry jam, kirsch and the half punnet of sliced fresh strawberries.

Pour the custard into the prepared base.

Top with the second round of dough, pinching the edges together around the sides.

Sprinkle the top with the caster sugar and bake at 190°C for 30-40 minutes, until the pastry is coming away from the sides of the tin and the top is turning golden brown.

Let the shortcake cool slightly in the tin before turning out.

Serve warm, with whipped cream and fresh whole strawberries.

Variation

A 425 g tin sliced peaches, drained; use ½ the peaches, chopped, in the filling and the rest, unchopped, as decoration. Use peach or apricot jam instead of the strawberry.

Fruit Compote

This very refreshing compote has a delightful flavour enhanced by the fresh fruit juice and a hint of cinnamon, while the almonds provide an excellent textural contrast.

1 tsp grated orange rind
½ cup fresh orange juice
1½ tsp grated lemon rind
2¼ tbsp fresh lemon juice
⅔ cup water
2 tbsp raisins
¾ cup chopped dessert figs
5 cm piece of cinnamon stick or ¼ tsp ground cinnamon
½ cup juice from stewed or tinned apricots
1 425 g tin of apricot halves, drained and chopped or equivalent fresh, stewed
1-2 medium bananas, sliced
⅓ cup whole blanched or unblanched almonds

Place the first 9 ingredients into a heavy-based medium saucepan.

Increase the heat and bring the mixture to the boil, stirring constantly.

Reduce heat and simmer gently, stirring occasionally, for 10 minutes.

Allow to cool a little, then pour over the chopped apricots in a serving bowl. Cool.

Cover and place in a refrigerator until very well chilled.

Just before serving, add the sliced bananas and the almonds.

Serve with ice cream, e.g. coffee ice cream (p. 138) and/or whipped cream.

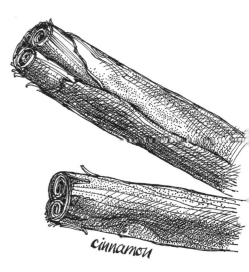

cinnamon

The many people who have begged for this recipe in the past are an indication of how popular this baked cheesecake is. It has a lovely light filling which rises like a souffle when cooking, but settles back down into the pan when cooled. The recipe will produce a large, rich cheesecake to serve 8-10 people — as long as they don't all want seconds!

This cake does not skewer test well; if a skewer comes out clean from the middle, it is overdone.
If the top starts to brown while cooking, cover gently with foil.

*Egg whites freeze very well. Just thaw them at room temperature before using.

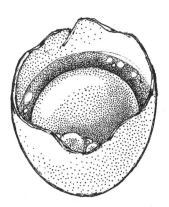

Sue's Very Special Baked Cheesecake

Crust
1 cup plain white flour
50 g chilled butter, chopped
¼ cup caster sugar
2 egg yolks (save these whites for another use)*
1 tsp vanilla

Place all the ingredients in a food processor and process just until the mixture begins to 'ball'. Remove the dough from the processor, pressing into the shape of a ball as you do so, then place in a clean plastic bag or in plastic wrap. Refrigerate for 30 minutes.
Heat the oven to 200°C.
Line the bottom of a greased 23 cm (9 inch) round cake tin with butter paper (or buttered greaseproof).
Roll or pat out the pastry to fit, then prick the pastry all over with a fork.
Bake at 200°C for 10 minutes, or until the pastry has turned light golden and seems fairly firm.

Filling
⅔ cup crushed pineapple, well drained (reserve ⅓ cup of the juice for the topping)
1½ cartons cream cheese (i.e. 375 g)
250 g sour cream
⅓ cup sugar
½ tsp cinnamon
1 tsp vanilla essence
2 drops almond essence (optional)
1 lemon, grated rind and juice
3 medium-large eggs (or 4 small), separated

Pre-heat the oven to 180°C.
Separate the eggs.
Place all the ingredients except the pineapple and the egg whites into the bowl of a food processor and process until smooth.
Place the egg whites into a clean bowl and whisk until they are stiff and 'peak'.
Stir the well-drained pineapple into the egg yolk mixture, then gently fold in the stiffly beaten egg whites.
Pour the filling mixture onto the cooked pastry in the cake tin, and bake at 180°C until set — 45 minutes should be correct, maybe a couple of minutes more. The top should feel firm to the touch when cooked (i.e. not wobbly).

Cool the cake, then chill in the refrigerator until it is well set. Turn out onto a plate. Remove the lining paper, then gently invert onto another plate so that it is right side up once more.

Topping

**170 g tin passionfruit pulp or ½ cup fresh, with ¼ cup sugar
added — heat to dissolve the sugar, then cool
2 tbsp lemon juice
⅓ cup of pineapple juice (reserved)
1 generous tbsp cornflour, mixed with 2 tbsp water**

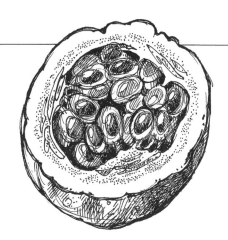

Put the passionfruit pulp, the lemon juice and the pineapple
juice into a saucepan.
Stir in the cornflour mixture and bring to the boil, stirring
constantly until thickened.
Cool, then pour over the cold cheesecake.
Chill until you are ready to serve.
Serve with whipped cream.

Variations

Other fruit combinations can be used, such as blueberries,
cherries, apricots, etc.
Drain an equivalent amount of juice as above fruit for the canned
or stewed fruit, reserve some juice.
Reserve some extra fruit for the topping (½ cup — instead of the
passionfruit pulp).
Proceed as for the pineapple/passionfruit cheesecake.

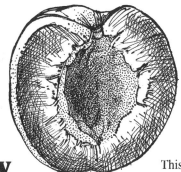

Fruit Flummery

**1 825 g tin apricots, drained, reserving ½ cup syrup or equivalent
fresh, stewed
2 tbsp gelatine or agar-agar
250 g carton of sour cream or yoghurt**

Sprinkle the gelatine over the reserved ½ cup of apricot
syrup.
Dissolve in a bowl over hot water or microwave for 40 seconds
on high.
Cool the gelatine mixture slightly.
Puree the apricots in a food processor.
Add the sour cream and gelatine and process until smooth.
Pour into a mould or serving bowl or individual parfait glasses
and refrigerate until set.

This simple flummery, which
takes only minutes to make,
is a light and refreshing
dessert which can be
presented in a number of
ways. Serve it layered with
ice cream or whipped cream
and fruit in parfait glasses, or
turn it out of a ring mould,
decorated with whipped
cream and chopped nuts. You
can make it look quite
impressive. We've used
apricots here, but any tinned
or fresh stewed fruit may be
used — plums are good, and
peaches, etc.

155

This dessert, with its sweet ginger and nut filling, is most unusual, rich and sumptuous. (A small piece of such a dessert is a perfect finish to a curry meal.)

Martinique Ginger and Almond Tart

Pastry

¾ cup wholemeal flour
½ cup plain flour
75 g cold butter, cut into cubes
3-4 tbsp cold water

Place the flours into a food processor. Add the cut up butter and process briefly, then pour in the water slowly. It should just start to form a 'ball'.
Wrap in plastic wrap and refrigerate for 30 minutes.
Pre-heat the oven to 200°C.
Roll out to fit a greased 23 cm (9 inch) flan tin with removable sides.
Line the pastry case with greaseproof paper or tin foil, making sure to cover the sides.
Fill with dried beans or uncooked rice (keep a jar full for this purpose) and bake at 200°C for 15 minutes.
Remove the beans and bake for 5 minutes more.

Filling

125 g butter
2½ cups brown sugar
1 cup ground almonds
2 tbsp skinned and grated fresh ginger
¼ cup cream
4 egg yolks (keep the whites for ice cream, pavlova, etc.)

In a heavy-based saucepan, gently heat the butter, brown sugar, the almonds, ginger and the cream.
Bring just to boiling point then turn the heat down. Simmer, stirring constantly for 8-10 minutes.
Remove from the heat and quickly beat in the eggs one by one. Use a whisk or beater to do this.
Cool the mixture slightly, then pour into the tart shell and return to a 180°C oven for 15 minutes.
Cool to room temperature.
Serve with ice cream or whipped cream.

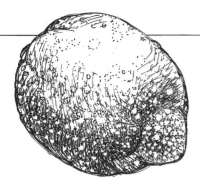

Ginger and Lemon Cheesecake

This cheesecake looks mightily impressive, and has a wonderful, refreshing flavour. A no risk, always popular dessert, it will serve 6-8 or more.

Base

185 g wine biscuits, crushed in a food processor
3½ tbsp margarine
½ tsp nutmeg

   Pre-heat the oven to 180°C.
Melt the margarine, then mix thoroughly with the crushed wine biscuits and the cinnamon.
Press firmly into a 20 cm (8 inch) round tin with a removable base.
Bake at 180°C for 10 minutes, no longer.
Remove from the oven and allow to cool.

Filling

1 cup boiling water
⅓ cup caster sugar
1½ tsp lemon rind, grated
4 tbsp lemon juice
1 tbsp minced fresh ginger (mince in processor)
1 tbsp very finely chopped crystallised ginger
2½ tbsp gelatine
1 410 g tin evaporated milk, very well chilled
1 cup caster sugar
½ cup cottage cheese
250 g cream cheese

   Place the water, sugar, lemon rind and juice, gingers and gelatine in a saucepan and heat slowly, stirring until the sugar is dissolved.
Bring just to boiling point, stirring occasionally, then remove from the heat and allow to cool (don't allow to set, though).
Beat the well-chilled evaporated milk with an electric beater until it has doubled in size and is thick and creamy (you will need a large bowl for this), adding the caster sugar in 3 lots as you do this.
Beat the cream cheese and the cottage cheese together in a separate bowl until smooth, then beat the cheeses into the evaporated milk mixture.
Now beat in the cooled gelatine mixture until it is well combined and pour into the cooled biscuit base.
Place in the refrigerator until set, at least 4 hours.

157

Miscellaneous

Samosas

1½ cups plain flour
¼ tsp salt
3 tbsp softened margarine or ghee
5-6 tbsp (⅓ cup) water

Place the flour and salt in a food processor bowl with the steel blade in place. Add the softened margarine, then process for a few seconds until the ingredients look like breadcrumbs. Using the pulse button, add the water until the dough starts to 'ball'. Don't over process, however.

or

sieve the flour and salt into a bowl, rub in the softened margarine or ghee, then mix in the water, a little at a time, until the dough begins to form into a ball.

Turn the dough onto a floured board and knead it for 5-10 minutes, until it loses any stickiness and gains an 'elastic' quality.

Place the dough in plastic wrap and set aside for 45 minutes to 1 hour.*

Knead the dough again, briefly, then form the dough into 20-24 balls.Roll each out quite thin, then cut in half and lay the 2 pieces one on top of the other.

Press these lightly together, then roll them out as thinly as possible in a semi-circle.

Place 2 teaspoonfuls (approximately) of the filling on one half of the pastry, moisten the edges and fold the other half over. Press the edges firmly together.

Deep fry the prepared samosas in hot oil until lightly golden. Drain on kitchen paper.

Samosas are served either hot or at room temperature. They can be made up to a day in advance, refrigerated in an airtight container and then reheated in a medium-hot oven for serving.

Samosas are delicious little stuffed pastries, which can be eaten any time as a snack, as part of a lunch or dinner, or served with drinks as an appetiser/entree.

The recipe for samosa filling is given on p. 112 as Potato and Green Pea Curry, so it seems unnecessary to repeat it here. You may wish to halve the curry recipe, however, as half will be sufficient to make the samosas.
Makes 20-24 samosas.

*Samosa dough may be made a day in advance and refrigerated at this stage. To freeze samosas, par-fry them, drain, then freeze in single layers. Defrost and fry a second time when required.

Tahini

1 cup sesame seeds
1 garlic clove, crushed
5 tbsp olive oil
2 tbsp lemon juice
½ tsp salt

Toast the sesame seeds, stirring, in a heavy-based frypan over a gentle heat until they are golden. Take care not to burn them. Or microwave on high for approximately 4 minutes, stirring twice.

Place the seeds into a food processor bowl with the metal chopping blade and blend until there are no seeds left whole. This step is most important; if the sesame seeds are not actually ground, the tahini will have very little flavour.

Add the garlic then, while the motor is still running, add the oil slowly, followed by the lemon juice and salt.

Tahini can be refrigerated for up to a week, or frozen.

Tahini is a sesame seed paste, Middle Eastern in origin. It's a very useful ingredient to have on hand if you enjoy experimenting with food, as it's often an essential ingredient in many recipes.* It has a lovely nutty taste from the toasted sesame seeds.

*See the recipe for Hummus, p. 160, and the recipe for Felafel, p. 160.

159

Hummus is very popular these days; not only does it taste good, but it's inexpensive and full of protein. Middle Eastern in origin, it's traditionally served as a spread or dip with pita bread (see p. 101) but you can of course serve it with French sticks or any bread, especially home-made.
You can also serve it with raw vegetables such as carrot or celery sticks, cauliflorets, capsicum strips, etc.
Add a variety of cheeses, more salads, and you have a meal.

*Cover the raw chickpeas (1 cup will produce 2 cups cooked) with cold water, soak for at least 2 hours or overnight; then pressure cook for 30 minutes or simmer for 1½-2 hours or pressure cook without pre-soaking for 45-50 minutes. Chickpeas usually shed their skins during cooking — without being obsessive about it, remove as many of these as you can easily manage, as they can impart a slightly bitter taste.
**Tahini (sesame seed paste) is available from specialty stores, but it's very easy to make your own (see p. 159).*

Felafel, or chickpea patties, are a very popular snack in the Middle East. They make a perfect accompaniment to cocktails, and can also be served in pita bread, with hummus or tahini, lettuce and tomato.

Hummus

2 cups cooked chickpeas (garbanzo beans)*
2 tbsp of reserved cooking water
4-6 cloves garlic, crushed
½ cup tahini**
½ cup lemon juice
1 tsp salt
1 tsp freshly ground pepper (measured!)
¾ cup chopped parsley
black olives and a sprig of parsley for garnish

Place the cooked chickpeas in a food processor with the 2 tbsp reserved cooking water and the remaining ingredients except the parsley.
Blend to a thick paste, then blend again, very briefly — just enough to mix.
Place in a serving dish, cover and refrigerate until needed, but it's nicest served at room temperature if possible.
Garnish with black olives and a sprig of parsley.

Felafel

225 g chickpeas (1¼ cups), soaked in water for 24 hours
1 medium onion, peeled and finely chopped
2 cloves garlic, crushed
1 slice wholemeal bread, crusts removed, torn and soaked in water
3 tbsp parsley, chopped
½ tsp ground cumin
½ tsp ground coriander
¼ tsp baking powder
1 tsp salt
¼ tsp chilli powder
½ tsp freshly ground black pepper
1 tbsp lemon juice

Place the rinsed and well-drained chickpeas in a food processor, then blend until they resemble coarse breadcrumbs.
Add the onion, garlic and bread with the water squeezed out.
Process until smooth, then add all the remaining ingredients and process briefly.
Turn the mixture into a bowl and allow to rest for 1 hour.
Mould into slightly flattened balls, about 2.5 cm (1 inch) across.
Deep fry for 3-4 minutes, turning once, or shallow fry in a large pan or wok containing about 2 cm (¾ inch) oil, turning once.
Drain on kitchen paper.
Serve hot.

chickpeas

Home-made Curry Powder

3 tbsp ground cinnamon
3 tbsp ground coriander
2 tbsp ground tumeric
2½ tbsp ground cumin seed
1 tbsp ground fenugreek
1½ tbsp dry mustard
1½ tbsp ground cardamom
1½ tbsp garlic salt
1½ tbsp poppy seeds
2 tbsp ground dried chillies
2 tbsp ground black pepper
1 tbsp ground ginger

Store in an airtight jar.
Mix well. Curry should always be sauteed in ghee, oil or butter before other ingredients, especially liquids, are added.

This curry powder is not a definitive recipe, but it is a quick and convenient basic one. The spices used to make a curry powder should really be bought whole, then freshly ground when needed. However, if you purchase fresh ground spices and don't keep them sitting around too long, this curry is a good substitute, and vastly superior to most commercial brands.

You can leave the chillies out of this recipe completely if you wish, or adjust the content accordingly. You do need to use more of this powder than the commercial kind — almost twice as much as a general rule, more if you omit the chillies.

Indian Puris and Chapatis

1 cup plain flour
1 cup wholemeal flour
1 tbsp oil
¾ cup warm water (approx.)
oil for deep frying

Place the flours in a bowl and mix well.
Add the oil to the warm water and mix this quickly into the flours using a knife.
Turn the dough out onto a lightly floured bench and knead until it is smooth, no longer sticks and has an 'elastic' tension. This should take about 7-10 minutes.
Return the dough to the bowl, cover with a damp cloth and leave in a warm place for 30 minutes (more, if you need it).
Divide into 16 pieces, then shape these into ball shapes.
Roll each ball out as thinly as possible, into a thin round pancake about 15 cm (6 inches) in diameter.
Deep fry in hot oil (at least 1.25 cm (½ inch) deep) for about 30 seconds on each side.
Drain on absorbent paper.

It is most unusual to find anyone, young or old, who doesn't like puris. Puris are one of the forms of bread eaten in curry-eating countries. They are deep fried, puffed and light, simple to make and well worth the effort. Most often served instead of rice, they are torn and wrapped around the curry, using the fingers; but rice may be also served. For chapatis, see note below.*

To make chapatis use the puri recipe but cook in a heavy-based, ungreased frypan instead of deep frying — otherwise the procedure is exactly the same. A good idea is to use half the above dough to make chapatis first; then pour in some oil and make puris for the same meal.

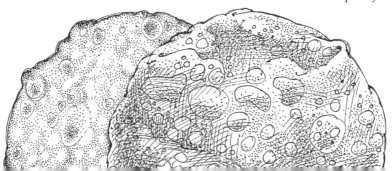

Raitas and sambals (side dishes) can help make a curry become an exotic and sumptuous feast; don't forget, though, that they may be served with other meals as well. See also the Plum or Prune Raita and the Celery and Apple Sambal (p. 113), the Grape and Banana Raita and the Tomato and Onion Sambal on p. 115 and Cucumber and Capsicum Raita on p. 111. Don't forget a selection of chutneys, too, such as Green Mango Chutney (p. 171), as side dishes.

Raitas and Sambals

Raw Zucchini and Mint Raita with Cashews

2 small zucchini, cut into thin strips lengthwise
1 tbsp good mint sauce
2 tbsp cashew nuts, roughly chopped and toasted
1 cup plain yoghurt
⅛ tsp of nutmeg
⅛ tsp cinnamon
½ tsp salt

Stir all ingredients together just before serving. Serve at room temperature.

Cabbage and Coconut Sambal

2 tsp butter or margarine
1 small onion, peeled and chopped fine
¼ medium cabbage, coarsely chopped
1 tsp sugar
salt and freshly ground pepper to taste
¼ tsp chilli pepper
1 tbsp lemon juice
¼ cup cream
¼ cup coconut, toasted

All these steps can be cooked in a microwave.

Heat the butter gently and saute the onion until clear and soft.
Stir in the cabbage, sugar, salt and pepper, chilli pepper, lemon juice and the cream.
When the cabbage is wilted and softening, add the toasted coconut.
Cool and serve at room temperature.

Prunes in Yoghurt

1½ cups natural yoghurt
½ cup stoned, chopped prunes

Mix the yoghurt and the prunes together and serve in a small deep bowl.

Nuts

A simple side dish of roasted nuts is always appreciated as an accompaniment to a curry. Peanuts will do, or a mixture.

Onion and Capsicum Sambal

2 medium-sized onions, peeled and finely sliced
1 clove garlic, crushed
1 small capsicum, seeded and finely sliced
juice of 1 lime or lemon
salt and freshly ground pepper to taste

Mix all the ingredients together, add the lime or lemon juice and season to taste.

Fresh Apple Chutney

¼ cup desiccated coconut
½ cup hot milk
2 tbsp salt
cold water
2 large green apples
2 tbsp onion, finely chopped
2 tbsp capsicum, finely chopped
juice of 1 lemon

Soak the desiccated coconut in the hot milk for 20 minutes, drain and discard the liquid.
Dissolve the salt in a bowl of hot water.
Peel, core and chop the apples small; place in the bowl of salted water, then let stand for 10 minutes.
Drain the apples, mix with the onion, capsicum and well-drained coconut.
Sprinkle with the lemon juice, toss and serve immediately.

Fresh Peach and Orange Sambal

2 fresh peaches, skinned, stoned and chopped
1 orange, peeled and chopped, plus any juice which threatens to escape in the process
½-¾ cup sour cream
1 spring onion, with green leaves, chopped finely

This sambal should be prepared just before serving if possible, so that the peaches don't brown.
Mix the prepared peaches and orange with the sour cream, then garnish with the finely chopped spring onion.

163

Do It Yourself Yoghurt

Yoghurt is so versatile. It's great for breakfast or dessert with fresh fruit, of course, but is also a valuable nutritive addition to savoury meals. Use it as a garnish for soups and mix it to create raitas (yoghurt-based side dishes) for curries, etc. Eat it as a snack or as an accompaniment to main meals, Middle Eastern style.

All utensils used to prepare yoghurt should be scrupulously clean.

6 cups milk
¾ cup milk powder (either full cream or low fat)
⅓ cup natural sweetened or unsweetened yoghurt

Place the milk and the milk powder in a large saucepan. Using an egg beater or whisk, mix well.
Bring the milk just to boiling point, then remove it from the heat.

Cool the mixture until it is just above blood heat. If you dip in your (very clean) little finger, it should tingle but not feel hot. If it feels cool, the mixture is too cold.

This yoghurt can be used to start another batch . . . and so on . . . and so on . . .

Take a little of the milk from the saucepan and mix it with the yoghurt. Add this yoghurt/milk mixture to the saucepan.
Pour the contents of the saucepan into a bowl (preferably plastic). Place a plate on top of the bowl then wrap a towel around it.
Leave the wrapped bowl in a warm place, such as on top of a hot water cylinder, for 6 hours. Unwrap it, then place it in the refrigerator to keep (or use it straightaway).

Dressings and Sauces

Basic Vinaigrette

⅔ cup olive or vegetable oil (olive is best)
⅓ cup lemon juice or vinegar (wine or cider)
¾ tsp salt
½ tsp freshly ground black pepper

Place all the ingredients in a jar with a screw-on lid and shake well to combine.
Variations

1. Garlic Vinaigrette
Add 2-3 cloves crushed garlic.

2. Mustard and Garlic
Add 2-3 cloves crushed garlic and 1 tsp prepared mustard, such as Dijon.

3. Herb
Simply place a sprig of tarragon, basil or any fresh herb of your choice into the jar of dressing and allow it to impart its flavour (can be left for 4-5 days) or chop 1 tbsp leaves finely, add to the basic dressing and shake well.

A vinaigrette is largely a matter of taste; this basic recipe gives very traditional proportions and will suit most people well. Adjust the proportions of oil and lemon to suit yourself, however. For example, many people prefer a sharper dressing and would therefore increase the amount of lemon juice to ½ cup or even more.

More than one variation may be used.

Sesame Dressing

3 tbsp olive or vegetable oil
2 tbsp lemon juice
salt and freshly ground pepper to taste
1 tsp honey
3 tbsp toasted sesame seeds
1 clove garlic, crushed (optional)

Place all ingredients in a jar with a screw-on lid. Shake well to blend.

Oriental Dressing

6 tbsp soya sauce
⅓ cup finely chopped orange peel
¼ cup red wine vinegar
½ cup oil
1 tbsp toasted sesame seeds
1 tbsp fresh ginger, skinned and minced
2 tbsp peanut butter
2 tsp sugar

Place in a blender or processor and blend until all the ingredients are combined.

If you like garlic you'll love aioli as a dressing for salads or as a dip for raw carrot and celery sticks, etc.

The 2 egg yolks can be replaced by 1 egg, but this will detract from the texture and flavour of the dressing, especially if you want it for something special.
We suggest putting egg whites in a small covered container and freezing them. Use them for a pavlova (p. 148) or meringues (p. 145) for example, thawed at room temperature.

Aioli

4 large cloves garlic, peeled and crushed
2 tbsp lemon juice
2 egg yolks*
1 tbsp fresh parsley
½ tsp salt
some good grinds of black pepper
1 cup olive oil

Place all the ingredients except the oil into a food processor or blender until well combined.
Slowly add the olive oil in a steady stream, while the motor is still running. This must be done without haste; the oil should be no more than dribbled in.
When finished, the mixture should be thick and creamy.

Basic Mayonnaise

Follow the Aioli Dressing recipe, omitting or reducing the garlic and the parsley. Use 1 egg instead of the 2 yolks unless the mayonnaise is of particular importance in the recipe; the lemon juice may be replaced by white or wine vinegar if you don't have lemon juice on hand.

Herb Mayonnaise

We use this as an all-purpose dressing, or dip for crudites — children and adults love it (children who don't particularly like vegetables seem to love this with raw carrot sticks, for example). It's great on sandwiches or crackers with cheese, combined with sliced tomato, cucumber, etc.
Use the recipe for aioli, but use 2-3 average cloves of garlic, 1 whole egg instead of the 2 yolks, and replace the lemon juice with cider vinegar if you wish.
Add ⅓ cup parsley, plus ⅛ of 1 onion, peeled, plus 2 tbsp fresh herbs such as French tarragon, oregano, a little mint, basil, or similar, stalks removed.
Chop until all the ingredients are well blended, before adding the oil very slowly.

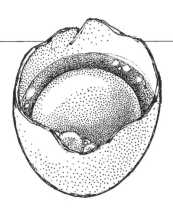

Easy Hollandaise Sauce

4 egg yolks
1 tbsp lemon juice
1 tsp Dijon style mustard
½ tsp salt
freshly ground pepper to taste
125 g butter, melted

Place the egg yolks in a food processor or blender with the lemon juice, mustard, salt and pepper.
Heat the butter in a saucepan (or microwave) until bubbling.
Blend the yolks briefly, for about 5 seconds. With the motor still running, add the butter in a thin stream until it is thickened.
Adjust the seasoning, and reheat gently to serve.

This classic sauce is very quickly and easily made using a food processor or blender. It's wonderful spooned over perfectly cooked cauliflower or broccoli, for example, and is also very nice served over poached eggs — in fact you won't have any trouble in inventing uses for it.
Freeze the egg whites if you don't want to use them immediately, and any leftover sauce can also be frozen in a covered container.

Fresh Tomato Sauce

500 g fresh tomatoes, peeled and chopped or use a 420 g tin whole peeled tomatoes, drained and chopped
1 tsp dried sweet basil or 1 tbsp fresh chopped
1 tsp brown sugar
1 tbsp butter or margarine
1 tsp salt
¾ tsp freshly ground black pepper (measured!)

Place all the ingredients into a saucepan, and bring to the boil. Reduce the heat and simmer gently for 15 minutes.
Pass through a sieve, pressing down gently to extract all the liquid.
Reheat if necessary.

This sauce is quick, easy and very useful for serving on steamed vegetables, plain rice, pasta, savoury crepes, vegetable loaves, etc.

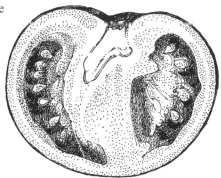

Pickles, Relishes and Chutneys

You can always justify any time spent in making pickles, relishes and chutneys by the fact that it saves you time later on. Served with home-made bread or French sticks, a selection of cheeses, a salad, some hard-boiled eggs perhaps, and some fresh fruit — and there you have a lunch to delight any guest, but which takes you hardly any time at all to prepare.

and

if you've got pickle and cheese to go with cracker biscuits, who needs to bake much?

and

sandwiches aren't nearly so boring when you can add a dash of relish to your cottage cheese and coleslaw or whatever . . .

These sweet-sour gherkins are simple to do, and extremely popular. It's not advisable to double the recipe, though; it's best to make 2 separate lots (otherwise they may shrivel).

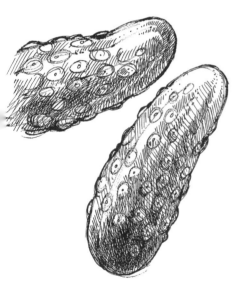

Gherkins

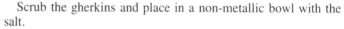

1½ kg small fresh gherkins
¼ cup salt
1 bay leaf
1 5 cm stick of cinnamon
4 whole cloves
2 small dried chillies
1 tsp peppercorns
6 cloves garlic, peeled and chopped in half
4 cm piece of fresh root ginger, peeled and chopped into 3 pieces
4 cups malt vinegar
1½ cups sugar

Scrub the gherkins and place in a non-metallic bowl with the salt.
Leave, stirring occasionally, for 3-5 hours. Drain.
Place all the spices, the garlic, ginger, vinegar and the sugar in a large preserving (jam) pan and bring to the boil. Stir regularly.
Add the drained gherkins and bring back to the boil — this should take about 5 minutes. Simmer 1 minute, then remove the pan from the heat.
Remove the gherkins from the spiced vinegar, and pack into clean, hot jars.
Pour the liquid over the gherkins, so that the smallest gap is left at the very top of the jars.
Cover with plastic screw-on tops which have had boiling water poured over them and then been left for 5 minutes.
Store for at least 3 weeks before using.
This recipe makes 2 1 litre jars.

Eddie's Courgette Pickle

3 kg courgettes
1½ cups peeled, sliced onions
2-3 large garlic cloves, skinned but left whole
⅓ cup salt
3 cups sugar
1½ tsp tumeric
1½ tsp celery seed
2 tbsp mustard seed
3 cups white vinegar

Wash the courgettes, then drain and cut into 6 mm (¼ inch) slices. Halve or quarter these according to the size of your courgettes.
In a large bowl, combine the courgette slices, the onions, garlic and the salt.
Allow to stand for 3 hours, mixing occasionally.
Drain off the liquid and remove the garlic. Combine the sugar, tumeric, celery and mustard seeds with the vinegar in a jam pan or similar. Bring to the boil, stirring regularly. Add the drained courgette/onion mixture and heat through to a simmer, allowing 7 minutes in all.
Pack loosely in clean hot jars, leaving a 1 cm gap at the top.
Place seals which have been heated (pour boiling water over them and leave for 5 minutes) on the jars. Screw on the screw band, but do not tighten.
Process in a water bath, large pot or pressure cooker for 10 minutes. Jars should sit on crumpled foil to deflect direct heat if you do not have a water bath. Time from when the water (just covering the jars) starts to boil.
Remove and tighten lids.

This pickle is always in demand as it tastes so good and is so versatile — delicious on biscuits with cottage or cheddar cheese, in sandwiches, or just as an adjunct to a simple lunch with cheeses and home-made breads.

It's nice to make it with a mixture of green and yellow courgettes, although this makes no difference to the taste; you can also use medium thin-skinned cucumbers (seeded) instead of the courgettes.
Although you can happily use large courgettes, if you're using those which have grown to small marrow size you will have to scoop out the seeds before using.

Easy Pickled Onions

1200 ml malt vinegar (or white as you prefer)
250 g honey
1 tsp black peppercorns
1 tsp skinned, grated fresh ginger
2-4 small dried red chillies, left whole (optional)
1.5 kg small pickling onions

Place all the ingredients except the onions into a large saucepan and bring to the boil, stirring.
Simmer gently, covered, for 5 minutes, then remove from the heat and allow to cool.
Peel the onions by pouring boiling water over them and leaving for approximately 40 seconds. Tip them into a basin of cold water and you'll find that the skins slip off quite easily.
Pack the peeled onions firmly into very clean jars, which have been washed then heated in an oven for 10 minutes or more at 110°C.
Screw on clean lids (to clean — cover with boiling water and leave for 5 minutes) and leave the onions to mature for at least a week before you sample them.

This recipe is also very old, and has withstood the test of time. Many recipes for pickling onions are unnecessarily complicated and, to add insult to injury, produce onions which are not crisp!

This is one of those recipes which has its origins somewhere over the last 2 generations. We felt that the original instructions (a panful of this and a saltspoon of that) were just a little too arbitrary, so it's now been defined. It can be eaten with just about anything you can imagine.

This relish has a 'bite' but isn't really hot, and the number of chillies can be reduced if you wish.

It's convenient to chop the onions and tomatoes in the evening, then leave them overnight ready for a fresh start in the morning.

If you manage to make only one chutney in a year, make this one — it's wonderful. Use it in sandwiches or on crackers with cottage cheese, fresh tomatoes, dill pickles or cheddar. We haven't yet met anyone who hasn't liked it and wanted the recipe, but for the uninitiated the amounts of fresh ginger, garlic and chillies may seem a bit daunting.

Don't change these amounts; make half the mixture if you feel unsure about it. The chutney has a jam-like consistency but a definite piquancy — it's not hot, though. If you do make the full amount, you need a larger container than a jam pan (a very large pot big enough to hold litre jars is ideal).
Yield is approximately 14 jars.

Venerable Tomato Relish

3 kg ripe tomatoes, chopped roughly
6 large onions, skinned and sliced
¼ cup salt
2 cups white sugar
7-10 small dried chillies, crushed
1 tbsp commercial curry powder
600 ml malt vinegar
1½ tbsp mustard powder
½ tsp cayenne pepper (optional)
1½ tbsp cornflour

Place the prepared tomatoes and onions in a plastic container, sprinkle with the salt and leave for 4 hours or overnight. Drain off the resulting liquid thoroughly, then place in a jam pan or similar.
Add the rest of the ingredients and boil for 30 minutes, stirring regularly.
Add the cornflour, mixed smooth with a little vinegar. Boil for another 5 minutes, then pour into clean heated jars.
Cover with sealing wax and cellophane, or plastic screw-on tops which have had boiling water poured over them and have been left for 5 minutes.

Mrs Fernando's Sri Lankan Chutney

5 kg fresh red tomatoes
140 g garlic, skinned
140 g fresh root ginger, skinned
7-8 g small dried chillies (about 40)
2 tsp salt
2 tsp cumin
1 tsp cinnamon
1 tsp ground cloves
1875 ml (2½ bottles) malt vinegar
4½ kg white sugar

Blanch the tomatoes in boiling water for a few minutes, then remove the skins. Chop roughly and simmer in their own juice for 20 minutes.
Chop the skinned garlic and ginger with the chillies in a food processor until fine.
Add to the tomatoes.
Next add the salt, spices and vinegar. Bring to the boil, then add the sugar and bring back to the boil.
Simmer until the mixture reaches a jam-like consistency (1½ hours approximately) stirring regularly.
Test as for jam.
Pour into clean sterilised jars and seal with wax and cellophane covers or with plastic screw-on lids which have had boiling water poured over them and have then been left for 5 minutes.

170

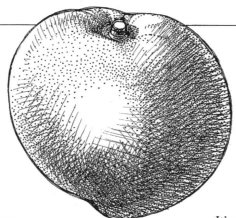

Green Mango Chutney

1 kg green mangoes
salt
24 small dried chillies (or more)
60 g garlic, crushed
60 g fresh root ginger
750 g brown sugar
250 g white sugar
600 ml malt vinegar
40 g mustard seeds

It's sometimes difficult to get mangoes and especially green mangoes (the best are those which are still hard but the flesh of which is turning yellow). Some people will be able to get them, however, so we feel the recipe is well worth including as it is so good.

Peel and slice the mangoes fairly small, discarding the stones.
Sprinkle them with salt and leave, covered, in a warm dry place for 24 hours.
Drain well.
Place the chillies, garlic and ginger in a food processor bowl and chop until very fine.
Place the sugars, vinegar, chillies, garlic, ginger and mustard seed in a large saucepan or jam pan and boil until the syrup thickens, about 30 minutes.
Add the rinsed and drained mangoes and simmer until they are tender, about 1-1½ hours.
Place a little of the chutney on a saucer and leave to cool for a few minutes. Nudge the top of the chutney with a fingertip; if the surface wrinkles, then the chutney is ready.
Pour into clean, hot, sterilised jars and either cover with sealing wax and then cellophane covers or with screw-on lids which have had boiling water poured over them and have been left for 5 minutes.

This particular marmalade evolved from experiments with a number of recipes, and has proved very successful — and popular.

Since you don't have to soak the fruit overnight, this marmalade is straightforward and easy to make. You can chop the fruit in just a few seconds with a food processor, although you will of course end up with a more finely chopped product than if you do this by hand. As long as you don't allow the fruit to 'mush' however, it's perfectly acceptable even to those of us who prefer a coarser cut.

*Setting point is usually indicated by placing a small amount (about ½ tsp) of the test mixture on a saucer, allowing to cool for a few minutes, then nudging it gently with a finger. If the surface of the marmalade wrinkles, as if it has a skin on top of it, then it has reached setting point.

Dark Ginger Marmalade

1½ kg fruit — use any combination of oranges and grapefruit you wish (or mandarins)
2 lemons
30 g root ginger, skinned (optional)
3½ litres (7 pints) water
250 g preserved ginger
3 kg sugar
2 tbsp treacle
2 tbsp whisky (optional)

First, halve all the fruit and squeeze out the pips and the juice into a bowl with a muslin cloth over it to catch the pips and reserve the juice.
Tie the pips and root ginger in the muslin, making a small bag. Now, cut the squeezed fruit finely or cut each half into 4 pieces and chop in a food processor.
Place the chopped fruit in a jam pan with the water, juice and the muslin bag containing the pips and the root ginger.
Simmer until the peel is quite soft and the volume has been reduced by approximately half — this should take 1½-2 hours.
Then remove the muslin bag, add the finely chopped preserved ginger, the sugar and the treacle.
Stir until the sugar has dissolved, simmer until setting point is reached, *then add the whisky (if used).
Pour into clean hot jars and either pour melted sealing wax over when it cools a little, then top with jam covers or cover with plastic screw-on tops which have had boiling water poured over them and have then been left for 5 minutes.
Makes approximately 8-9 jars.

Definitive Pastry (Short Crust)

The amounts given here provide sufficient for a single layer 23 cm (9 inch) pie or flan base. Simply double the recipe if you are making a double crust pie.

½ cup wholemeal flour
½ cup plain flour
¼ cup grated cheese
½ tsp salt
50 g very cold butter
¼ cup very cold water (approx.)*

Place all ingredients except the butter and the water in a food processor bowl.
Dice the butter and place on top of the other ingredients.
Process using the pulse control, adding the water slowly as you do so. (You may not need to use the full amount of water.) Three-four quick pulses should be all you need before the mixture starts to 'ball'.
Now press the moistened crumbs into a ball with your fingers and place in a plastic bag or wrap. Refrigerate for at least 30 minutes if time permits.
Roll out on a floured board to fit a 23 cm (9 inch) flan tin or similar.

Having tried just about every possible combination of plain/wholemeal flour proportions, butter/cheese content, etc., we've opted for this pastry recipe as the best all-purpose short crust. It can be used as a quiche or flan base and for both savoury or sweet dishes.

Other pastries given in this book are geared to specific recipes; this is a basic recipe and as such can be adapted according to need. If the pastry is to be used for a dessert, omit the cheese and instead add 10 g more butter (i.e. make up to 60 g).

If you don't keep cold water in your refrigerator, place an ice cube in tap water for a few minutes.

Nutty Square

1 cup wholemeal flour
1 cup coconut
½ cup sunflower kernels (optional)
¾-1 cup sultanas
2 cups rolled oats
¾ cup sugar
½ cup wheatgerm
½ cup sesame seeds
250 g butter
1 large tbsp honey or golden syrup
1 tsp baking soda

Pre-heat the oven to 160°C.
Mix the dry ingredients in a large bowl. Melt the butter and golden syrup together. Add the baking soda, then quickly stir into the dry ingredients.
Spread into a greased swiss roll tin or similar.
Bake at 160°C for 30-45 minutes.
Cut into squares when almost cool.

This square is a favourite with both adults and children. Not only does it contain healthy ingredients, but it's quick, easy to make and tastes great.

173

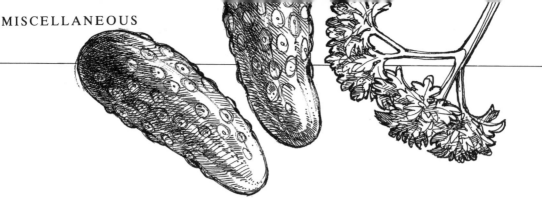

This is basically a scone type mixture, but it has a lovely savoury flavour and keeps well. Serve it buttered, with cheese or with chutneys, pickles or jam.

Serve it instead of a bread for lunch; it's good in cut lunches, too.

Cheese, Gherkin and Herb Loaf

1 cup plain flour
1 cup wholemeal flour
2 tsp baking powder
½ tsp prepared mustard such as Dijon
1 tsp salt
½ tsp freshly ground black pepper
¼ tsp cayenne pepper
75 g butter
1 cup grated cheddar cheese
1 heaped tbsp fresh chopped herbs, such as tarragon, or oregano
or 1 tsp dried
1 tbsp finely chopped parsley
3 gherkins (thumb size) chopped fine
1 egg
1 cup milk

Pre-heat the oven to 190°C.
Place the flours, baking powder, mustard, seasonings, and cayenne pepper into a food processor. Cut the butter into 4 and place on top of the other ingredients. Process briefly until the mixture is crumbly, then turn into a bowl.
Add the cheese, herbs and chopped gherkins.
Beat the egg lightly and add the milk.
Stir into the dry ingredients to make a soft dough.
Line the bottom of a greased loaf tin with butter paper or buttered greaseproof paper.
Pour the mixture into the prepared tin and spread evenly, pushing well into the corners.
Bake at 190°C for 40-50 minutes, or until a skewer inserted into the middle of the loaf comes out clean.

Fruit Cake

250 g butter
2½ cups plain flour
1 cup wholemeal flour
2 tsp baking soda
1½ kg mixed dried fruit
2 eggs
300 ml milk, brought to the boil then cooled in a sink of cold water
to warm temperature
2 tsp grated lemon rind
1 dsp grated orange rind
¼ cup fresh orange juice
125 g (about ½ cup) marmalade
whole almonds and/or glace cherries for decoration if desired
¼ cup brandy or sherry (optional)

This fruit cake could be made for Christmas or anytime as a substantial, delicious fruit cake. It's very economical and simple to make. It contains no sugar, but the inclusion of marmalade and the proportion of dried fruits ensure that it is quite sweet enough.

Pre-heat the oven to 120°C.
Rub or cut the butter into the flours and baking soda until the mixture resembles breadcrumbs.
Stir in the mixed fruit, making sure there are no 'clumps' of fruit, and that it is all well coated with flour.
Beat the eggs lightly, then add them to the dry ingredients with the boiled milk, lemon rind, orange rind and juice, and the marmalade.
Grease a 20 cm (8 inch) square cake tin and line the bottom of it with 2 layers of butter paper.
Pour the prepared mixture into the tin, hollowing it slightly in the middle and pressing well into the corners.
Press whole almonds and/or glace cherries gently onto the surface of the cake if you don't intend to ice it.
Bake in a slow oven for 4 hours at 120°C.
Allow to cool in the tin for 20 minutes, then turn out onto a cake rack.
Prick the cake all over the top with a skewer and pour over the brandy or sherry if desired, while the cake is still hot.

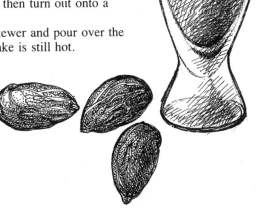

Index

177